GIUSEPPE UNGARETTI SELECTED POEMS

D1595332

SELECTED POEMS

Giuseppe

TRANSLATED, ANNOTATED, AND WITH

AN INTRODUCTION BY

Andrew Frisardi

FARRAR, STRAUS AND GIROUX

NEW YORK

Ungaretti

Farrar, Straus and Giroux

19 Union Square West, New York 10003

Translation, Introduction, and Notes copyright © 2002 by Andrew Frisardi
Italian poems copyright © 1942, 1943, 1945, 1947, 1948, 1949, 1954, 1961
by Arnoldo Mondadori Editore SpA, Milano

Printed in the United States of America

FIRST EDITION, 2002

Library of Congress Cataloging-in-Publication Data
Ungaretti, Giuseppe, 1888–1970.
   [Poems. English & Italian. Selections]
   Giuseppe Ungaretti : selected poems / Giuseppe Ungaretti ;
translated by Andrew Frisardi.— 1. ed.
     p. cm.
   ISBN 0-374-26075-3 (hc : alk. paper)
   1. Ungaretti, Giuseppe, 1888–1970—Translations into English. I. Title.

PQ4845.N4 A23 2002
851'.912 — dc21

2002020134

Designed by Quemadura

www.fsgbooks.com

10 9 8 7 6 5 4 3 2 1

FOR MY PARENTS, DARIO FRISARDI

AND MARIE SALLY CLEARY

Contents

Introduction: Giuseppe Ungaretti and the Image of Desolation   I x

FROM **L'ALLEGRIA/**

Joy (1931)   2

FROM **SENTIMENTO DEL TEMPO/**

A Sense of Time (1936)   70

FROM **IL DESERTO E DOPO/**

The Desert and After (1961)   152

FROM **IL DOLORE/**

Affliction (1947)   160

FROM **LA TERRA PROMESSA/**

The Promised Land (1950)   196

FROM **IL TACCUINO DEL VECCHIO/**

The Old Man's Notebook (1960);

DIALOGO/

Dialogue (1968);

AND **NUOVE/**

New Things (1970)   210

Ungaretti on Ungaretti (1 9 6 9)   2 3 9

Chronology   2 5 9

Notes   2 6 3

    L'ALLEGRIA / *Joy*   2 6 3
    SENTIMENTO DEL TEMPO / *A Sense of Time*   2 6 7
    IL DESERTO E DOPO / *The Desert and After* 2 7 5
    IL DOLORE / *Affliction*   2 7 5
    LA TERRA PROMESSA / *The Promised Land*   2 7 6
    IL TACCUINO DEL VECCHIO / *The Old Man's Notebook* 2 7 7
    DIALOGO / *Dialogue*   2 7 8
    NUOVE / *New Things*   2 7 8
    Ungaretti on Ungaretti   2 7 8

Acknowledgments   2 8 1

Index of Titles and First Lines   2 8 3

When I read a "hermetic" poet like Ungaretti, I often get the sense that his language has been pared by doubt, as if he felt that breaking the semantic threads of grammar would clear the way for a renewed sense of meaning in his doubting heart and mind. Or maybe his stitched-together fragments represent vestiges of faith or confidence in life's meaningfulness. Either way, it is an effort, and we feel the strain of it, of a religious sensibility to construct a cloister of language in a secular age.

Allegria di naufragi (Joy of Shipwrecks; 1919), Ungaretti's first full-length collection, established his reputation overnight as one of the leading Italian poets of his generation. Ungaretti's poetry was as new, strange, and, for many Italian readers, exciting as Eliot's "Prufrock" or Pound's *Mauberley* were to American and English readers of that period. As Eugenio Montale would say years later, the innovators of modernist poetry in Italy set out to "wring the neck of the old aulic eloquence"—namely, and immediately before them, the romanticism of Giosuè Carducci, the sentimental decadence of Giovanni Pascoli, and the bombastic decadence of Gabriele D'Annunzio. At the start of the 1910s the Crepuscular poets—most famously, Corrado Govoni, Sergio Corazzini, Guido Gozzano, and Marino Moretti—came out with their Jules Laforgue–influenced, ironic, subdued style, consciously breaking with the past augustness of the formidable Italian poetic tradition. Their vocabulary was that of everyday speech, their tone self-effacing, and their syntax free of inversions. The landscapes in their poetry were no longer the grandiose ones of Carducci or D'Annunzio, but rather, enclosed gardens and other domesticated spaces. Gozzano introduced modern neologisms into his poems: *fotografia, dagherròtipo,* and so on, as well as foreign words. The meter and rhyme schemes of the Crepusculars were less regular than Italian poets formerly had employed, and so their work was an important stage in the move toward *vers libre* in Italy.

An even more radical aesthetic, and one that Ungaretti also emulated in his early writing, was launched by Filippo Marinetti's *Futurist Manifesto,* which was published in 1912 in *Le Figaro* in Paris. The aspect of Marinetti's monomaniacal rant that had a special relevance for Ungaretti was his proposal of a new poetic language of *paroles en liberté,* joined in "ever deeper and distant analogical associations." Nineteen-twelve was the very year Ungaretti came to Paris, at age twenty-four, from his native city of Alexandria— interestingly, also Marinetti's home (although they didn't know each other there). French culture and education had been de rigueur in Alexandria ever since Napoleon occupied the city, so Ungaretti was completely bilingual from the start. His early immersion in authors such as Baudelaire, Rimbaud, Laforgue, and Mallarmé, rather than the more usual fare for Italian poets at that time, had everything to do with Ungaretti's decisive, innovative influence on Italian letters. Ungaretti came to Europe equipped for radical change. He immediately became an integral part of the intense creative ferment that was under way in Europe just before the war, as if in anticipation of the irreparable destruction that the war would inflict. As Ungaretti's close friend the Futurist Ardengo Soffici put it, the arts were breaking "with conventional forms in order to draw closer to the fluidity of life, to its impressions."

Ungaretti was in Paris for less than two years, but that was long enough for him to refer to that time, more than fifty years later, as his cultural and social coming-of-age. He attended Henri Bergson's and other lectures at the Sorbonne, became a close friend of

Apollinaire, and came into regular contact with the major exponents of the avant-garde: Picasso, Georges Braque, Fernand Léger, Giorgio de Chirico, Max Jacob, and others. Having become friendly with the Futurists Giovanni Papini, Aldo Palazzeschi, and Soffici, he was invited to collaborate with them on their new journal, *Lacerba*, where Ungaretti first published his poems. *Lacerba*, edited in Milan, and *La Voce*, in Florence, were the main organs for the earliest stages of Italian modernism.

As always, although Ungaretti was in the thick of cultural activity and public discourse about it, he went his own way. Like all of the most talented modernists, he was as much at odds with the avant-garde as he was a part of it. He was iconoclastic only to the extent that cultural detritus and insincere formalism were in the way of reality. The essence of language, the quasi-mystical resonance of the authentic poetic line, could be rediscovered only by starting over again with its basic units: the syllable, word, or phrase. Ungaretti was separated from his Futurist and Crepuscular peers by his moral seriousness and philosophical fervor: "While I did not use the word except when it came to me infused with moral content," he wrote in old age, "they . . . asked nothing of the word but a physical impressionability." Another way of saying this is that Ungaretti remained a committed humanist, as demonstrated, for instance, by his apprenticeship to Petrarch and Leopardi. He always defended culture, even as he acknowledged its transience and illusoriness. For Ungaretti, cultural forms, though always in need of renewal, are all there is at times between us and a terrifying emptiness. Such a humanistic stance would put Ungaretti at odds with the French Surrealists and with Freudian reductionism. Ungaretti would always espouse, as he put it, a waking dream, *un sogno ad occhi aperti*, rather than the somnambulism of the Surrealists. In an essay on Paul Valéry he wrote: "Valéry learns from Poe that in order to understand the genesis of a work of art one must start, not with an initial emotion, but from the technical means put to work by the artist to produce such and such an effect." For Ungaretti, this classical perspective would always be a safeguard against solipsism and aesthetic decadence. His summary statement about Valéry could also be said of him: "to utmost turbulence he opposed . . . utmost precision."

Just after Italy's entry into World War I in 1915, Ungaretti (who had already enlisted in the army) was sent to the Carso, in northern Italy, scene of some of the war's bloodiest battles. The immediate crisis of the war, of witnessing and being so close to death day after day, was the alembic in which Ungaretti's developing sensibility was purified. Not only did he lack the time to second-guess the amazing phrases that he jotted down as they came into his head, but he had every reason to believe that no one would ever read them (see Ungaretti's account of this in the notes section for *L'allegria* on pages 264–265). He was no more likely to survive the almost daily battles on the Austrian front than was the friend he wrote about in "Veglia" (Vigil):

> An entire night
> thrown down
> beside a
> butchered
> companion with his
> grimacing
> mouth turned
> to the full moon
> with his congested hands
> thrust
> into my silence
> I wrote
> letters full of love

I have never held
so hard
to life

Or, as Ungaretti wrote in 1963: "The war suddenly revealed to me
the language [of my own voice as a poet]. That is, I had to speak
quickly because time was limited . . . I had to express in a few
words . . . an extraordinary intensity of meaning." We might say,
ignoring Ungaretti's dislike of psychology, that his ego had noth-
ing left to grasp, nothing to lose. And in fact one of the most strik-
ing qualities of Ungaretti's war poems is the sense that the person
who spoke them is transparent; the "I" in them is closer to Taliesin
than to Petrarch.

When I find
a word
in this my silence
it is dug into my life
like an abyss

Or:

I waver
at the corner of a road
like a firefly

To say nothing of his famous minimalist gem, "M'illumino / d'im-
menso," which literally means something like "I turn luminous
in an immensity of spaces." When Ungaretti refers to himself
as "Ungaretti / man of pain," *uomo di pena*, the directness moves
us not because of one individual's suffering, but because an or-
dinary soldier's oblique identification with Christ, the universal
man, consecrates the massive suffering and death that war in-
flicts.

As a student of Bergson, Ungaretti had received philosophical justification for his natural proclivity for a knowledge that is global and immediate, intuitive, reaching into the essences of things by sympathy. As Glauco Cambon expressed it in his excellent long essay on Ungaretti, "The basic conception underlying Ungaretti's poetry is that of the existence of a universal, cosmic life to which man is integrally joined in a nonrational, intuitive way." Ungaretti, like many of the most forceful modernist poets, had a basically religious notion of his poetic calling: he wanted to "free the word from its conventional superstructures so that it might regain its original pristine form," so that it might, he said, "penetrate into one's darkest recess, without upsetting or being able to uncover its secret." Hence the distinction Ungaretti liked to make, following Leopardi, between the two Italian words for "word"—*parola* and *vocabolo*—the latter referring to literal meanings, the former to a word's ineffable essence. Ungaretti was quite explicit about his religious conception of poetry: "It is the search to establish a relationship with the inviolable secret within the divine creatrix." In his 1964 lectures at Columbia about his late poem "Canzone," Ungaretti said that the moments the poet can be a poet are exactly those when the "primal image" "ruptures the ice" of habitual daily consciousness. And in a 1965 interview he said that his early war poems were an attempt to close the gap between language and that which one would like to say. "Such a poetry," writes scholar Giusy Oddo, "annuls the distance between word and object, between word and image, its sense being captured in a spark of intuition." A literary label for this aesthetic is, of course, Hermeticism (actually coined in 1936 by Francesco Flora, a critic who considered Ungaretti's elliptical style too mannered). Hermetic poetry was a poetry that sought not to describe or represent, but to evoke. Some of the Italian poets, besides Ungaretti, who are considered hermetic are Montale, Salvatore Quasimodo, Alfonso Gatto, and Leonardo Sinisgalli. The Hermeticists were never a "school," as such; they were simply some poets who shared, in their very different ways, an aspiration toward "pure poetry."

· · ·

After Ungaretti left Alexandria and started to discover his ancestral roots in Italy and his cultural and intellectual roots in Paris, there would be no turning back: he would remain, as he put it, a man with many homelands. It could be said that Italy for him was the land of the fathers—his own paternity and Italy's poetic patrimony—while Alexandria was maternal, less linked in his imagination to the masculine creators of culture than to the enveloping maternal world of sustaining imagination and unfathomable mystery.

> In a bay in Alexandria there was discovered . . . , sunken in water, an ancient port, the primitive port of Alexandria: a buried harbor, therefore. And then, the reason why this port has become the symbol of my poetry is easy to explain. There is a secret in us that the poet dives into, and reaching the port he discovers this secret, therefore coming to give that little bit that a man can give of consolation to the soul.

If the poems in *L'allegria* represented found objects retrieved from the maternal buried harbor, those of *Sentimento del tempo* (A Sense of Time; 1936), his second complete collection, embodied the beginning of his long experiment with the assimilation of the Italian poetic tradition. Ungaretti's impulse was part of a general need for reconstruction after the war. What this meant for literature was represented by Vincenzo Cardarelli's founding of *La Ronda* in 1919 in Rome, the express purpose of which was to promote a new classical style, "to reconnect [said *La Ronda*'s manifesto] to the greatest and most authentic Italian tradition, [which was] interrupted after Leopardi and Manzoni." For Ungaretti, then, the naked flashes of insight that characterized the poems of his first book needed to be filled out and grounded by the memory of history. Another way to say this is that Ungaretti now felt a need to further substantialize his poetic language. *Sentimento del tempo*, as its title states, was a return to the temporal dimension after the split-second flashes of the war poems. In a piece he wrote in 1930 for Turin's *Gazzetta del Popolo*, he describes how after the war he set to work on assimilating the Italian poets—Jacopone, Cavalcanti, Dante, Petrarch, Tasso, Leopardi, and others—not, he says, for literary research: "I was looking for the song in them . . . the song of the Italian language." And: "It was my heartbeat that I wanted to feel in harmony with the heartbeat of my betters from a desperately loved land."

Ungaretti's passionate attachment to Italy and his Italian roots also led him to adhere to Mussolini and Italian fascism, shortly after meeting him, when Mussolini was a leading socialist agitator and journalist, just before Italy entered the First World War. Ungaretti's belief in fascism lasted for many years, although he did eventually renounce it and was critical of some of its policies. The scholar Luciano Rebay has charted the progress and nature of Ungaretti's politics during this period by following letters exchanged by Ungaretti with his close friend Jean Paulhan, who from 1925 to 1940 was the editor of *La Nouvelle Revue Française*, an important literary magazine in France. What comes out of Rebay's analysis is this: while Ungaretti trusted Mussolini "without a shadow of a doubt," the basis of Ungaretti's position was his belief in Mussolini's version of fascism as a movement for gaining rights for exploited Italian workers, restoring order and self-respect to a badly fragmented postwar Italy, and preserving tradition in industrialized Italian society. At no point in Ungaretti's letters or other writings do we see the racism and imperialist power mania that Italian fascism increasingly represented and that eventually led to Mussolini's downfall. Ungaretti was patriotic, but he was too cosmopolitan and tolerant to be narrowly nationalistic. He was vocal about his opposition to racist laws—he got into some political trouble for this at one point—and his anger over social conditions was directed toward the wide gap between rich and poor in early-twentieth-century Italy. Rebay shows that Ungaretti believed passionately in a political system that would be "for the people" and thought fascism was the system that could best accomplish this, bringing about "a social order capable of guaranteeing dignified work for all in accordance with their aptitudes and talents, regardless of class." In other words, Ungaretti's *mussolinismo* was based on the years leading up to the March on Rome, in which Mussolini's main agenda was a populist and antibourgeois revolution. Clearly Ungaretti came to this view as the working-class son of emigrants from Tuscany. A very high proportion of Italian writers (95 percent, according to the notes section in the Mondadori edition of Ungaretti's collected essays, by Luciano Rebay and Mario Diacono) were attracted by Mussolini's "pararevolutionary, paraprogressive, antibourgeois" promises of social change, while at the same time Mussolini's achievements, his public works and so on, were widely admired in Europe and America. This was the context in which Ungaretti's publisher solicited a preface from Mussolini for the 1923 edition of *Il porto sepolto* (The Buried Harbor). The idealism of Ungaretti and many other Italian writers, not balanced by facing and/or knowing the dark side of Mussolini's career, resembled that of the well-meaning but grossly mistaken modernist artists and intellectuals who were attracted by revolutions that turned out to be communist tyrannies.

Ungaretti's aim as a poet, meanwhile, was to find a modern idiom, cadence, and meter for bringing together the present with *un antico strumento musicale*, thereby linking modern poetry with the Italian patrimony. Ungaretti turned especially to Petrarch, Tasso, and Leopardi as exemplars of the Italian hendecasyllabic line— the Italian equivalent of the iambic pentameter in English— which he called "the natural poetic measure of Italian speech." Thus we find, in *Sentimento*, in addition to the blunt, concrete diction of *L'allegria*, a modernist grandiloquence: broken syntactical units have been transformed into a more fluid, complex organization; instead of the first-person speaker in the present tense, there is an evocative use of the past tense; and staccato phrasing has become mellifluous speech. As if to announce the decisive change in style, Ungaretti opens his book with these (untranslatable) mind-bogglingly beautiful lines:

> Dall'ampia ansia dell'alba
> Svelata alberatura.
>
> [Out of daybreak's huge and restless hunger
> Trees—like masts—revealed.]

It is no wonder that in the thirties Ungaretti became one of the most admired writers in Europe: the poems in *Sentimento* are so richly textured and perfectly made, the emotion in them so focused and intense.

The twenties and early thirties were happy (if indigent) years for him: he and his wife lived in Marino, one of the *castelli romani*, the ancient hilltowns east of Rome, where, as Ungaretti said, the feel of a small Renaissance town in the country was still intact. They had children, a son and a daughter, and Ungaretti rediscovered his ancestral soul in the pastoral landscape. The classical deities were realities now.

> He landed on a waterfront where evening
> Was everlasting, thick with ancient spellbound trees,

And made his way in,
And a flutter of feathers
Loosened from the piercing palpitations
Of the scalding water
Called him back, and he thought he saw
(Fading, reflourishing)
A shade; climbing again,
He saw it was a nymph
Asleep on her feet, her arms around an elm.

In other poems, this glimpse of sensual, erotic innocence was as-
sociated with the childhood world of Africa:

No more now will I go off alone
Between the vast plain and the open sea,
Nor hear, from far-off ages, homely, clear,
Loosening in the limpid air, shrill sounds;
Nor will crazy fantasy go stripping nude
The acid graces,
Exalting them in fabled forms;
Nor will I pursue Diana
Stepping from the sparse palm grove
In a fleet gown of light . . .

There is an opalesque, polysemous effect in this strange and won-
derful poem that I have tried to carry over somehow in my trans-
lation. For Ungaretti does not merely draw on memory, personal
and collective; he attempts to reproduce its effects, as if the poem
itself were an *experience* of memory.

Another way Ungaretti turned to traditional forms during the
twenties was in his return to Catholicism. During Holy Week in
1928 he went on retreat at the monastery of Subiaco, where he re-
newed his commitment to his childhood faith and started work-

ing on the longest poem in *Sentimento*, "La pietà" (Mercy), an Ecclesiastes-like proclamation about the possible futility of all human endeavor, including writing poetry:

> I have peopled the silence with names.
>
> Have I ripped mind and heart to pieces
> To fall into servitude to words?
>
> I am king of phantoms.
>
> O dry leaves,
> Soul carried here and there . . .

In the second half of *Sentimento* he substitutes the naked nymphs of the African oasis and the woods of Marino with a search for meaning and moral depth. "The Bible, not classical mythology, is now his text," writes Glauco Cambon.

> What difference does sin make
> If it no longer leads to purity?
>
> The flesh can scarcely recollect
> A time when it was strong.
>
> The soul is used and foolish.
>
> God, consider our frailty.

Once *Sentimento* was written, the trajectory of Ungaretti's writing life was set. One of the last poems he wrote for the collection, "Auguri per proprio compleanno" (Greetings for His Own Birthday), reiterates the themes of lost youth and disillusioned aspiration. Just after Ungaretti wrote this poem, in 1935, he conceived the idea for *La terra promessa* (The Promised Land; 1950), his fourth collection, which explores these motifs in depth. Joseph Cary, in his fine study of Montale, Ungaretti, and Umberto Saba, rightly criticizes *Terra promessa* for being too mannered and "stiflingly concerned with literary precedent." It's not hard to understand why it should be so: there is no poetry without eros, without a healthy dose of paganism—without, as Blake put it, being of the devil's party. Ungaretti flirted with drying himself out on abstraction and idol-smashing. He was far too much of a poet to succeed, however, and so we have the actually very beautiful rarefactions of *Terra promessa*:

> That negligible bit of sand which slides
> Without a sound and settles in the hourglass,
> And the fleeting impressions on the fleshy-pink,
> The perishable fleshy-pink, of a cloud . . .

For me, the poems of *Terra promessa* are like exquisite alpine flora atop an ascetic crag. "Canzone," for example, probably Ungaretti's most hermetic poem, very beautifully depicts in time-lapse detail the change-over from night to dawn. Ungaretti's 1964 explication of this poem demonstrates how precise its images are. When he refers to the sunrise "enervating into rainbow echoes," for instance, the physical reality represented in the poem corresponds to how "we know reality only through echoes," and that "sunrise doesn't reveal a pure world, but a world that documents its own ruin." I was struck, when I first read this passage, by the implied reference to Ungaretti's experience in the war, documented in "Vanità" (Vanity), an early poem about watching the sun rise over the aftermath of a battlefield:

> Suddenly
> the lucid
> awesome
> vastness

is high
above the rubble

And the man
bent
over the sun-
shocked
water
finds
he's a shadow

Rocked and
gently
broken

Ungaretti's focus changed for several years between the time he conceived of *Terra promessa* and the time he actually wrote it. In 1936 he was offered the chair of Italian literature and language at the University of São Paulo. He and his family moved there, and just as Ungaretti was getting used to his new prestige, his world fell apart: first the death of his nine-year-old son from complications associated with appendicitis; then the death of his brother and, toward the end of his stay in São Paulo (he was hired to a professorship at the University of Rome in 1942, a position he would hold until his retirement), the outbreak of World War II and the occupation of Rome. The death of Antonietto, his son, stirred such desperate emotion that the resulting poetry was more violent and visceral than anything since the war poems, although combined now with the artfulness that Ungaretti had acquired:

The many, gigantic, jumbled, glaucous stones
Shuddering still within the hidden slings
Of suffocated elemental flames

Or in the terrible virgin torrents'
Headlong unappeasable caress—
Above the dazzling glare of sand, relentless
Along an empty horizon, remember?

The Brazilian wilderness provided images for nature in its ferocious, unrelentingly brutal aspect. This is very different from the poems in *L'allegria*, where the elements are usually portrayed as healing and restorative. The change of perspective makes sense, of course: the war was caused by man, while Antonietto's death was a result of natural law. As in Leopardi's famous poem "A Silvia," which was in fact a model for Ungaretti's poem "Tu ti spezzasti" (You Were Broken), nature is blamed for plundering innocence:

Happy grace,
You were not able not to break
Against a blindness so implacable
You simple breath and crystal,

Too human flash of light for the pitiless,
Savage, unrelenting, droning
Roar of a naked sun.

One of the most striking aspects of Ungaretti's work as a whole is that he so consistently, powerfully, and honestly writes about death. I can't think of another modern poet who faces death more nakedly and on so many levels, who struggles with it more, grieves over it, and works it into his overall philosophy of life. (Paul Celan comes to mind as another poet with this sort of courage in his work; Celan published a volume of translations from Ungaretti in 1968.) *Il dolore* (Affliction; 1947), where the above poem was published, is the collection in which Ungaretti most vividly combines personal grief with collective suffering. One part of the collection,

"Roma occupata" (Rome Occupied; the poems in the current selection that come from this section are "Nelle vene" [In Veins] and "Accadrà?" [Will It Come to Pass?]), confronts the reality of Rome during World War II: a cradle of Western civilization in the throes of violence and chaos. Ungaretti despairs over the breakdown of culture and humanitarian values, but ultimately affirms the power of creative human endeavor to survive the darker forces that always threaten it.

> May your sudden pinkish trace,
> Mother mind, ascend again,
> And return to amaze me;
>
> Come back to life, unhoped for,
> Measure inconceivable, peace;
>
> Make it so I, in the balanced landscape,
> May mouth again the sounds of artless speech.

Ungaretti's reading and translating of Góngora and Racine—in addition to his interpretation of Michelangelo and the Roman Baroque, which I refer to below (see the notes section of *Sentimento del tempo*, pages 268–272, for Ungaretti's essay on this subject)—had given him models for a refined but robust art that is haunted by a sense of emptiness and entropy.

●   ●   ●

Much has been said, and rightly so, about the connection between Ungaretti's search for geographical belonging and his "quest for essentialness" (as Cambon put it) in his poetry. Ungaretti's early poem about his Arab friend's suicide in Paris suggests that he could see himself in Mohammed Sceab's despair over having been uprooted:

> ... [he] no longer knew how
> to live
> in his people's tent
> where you hear the Koran
> being chanted
> while you savor your coffee
>
> And he didn't know how
> to set free
> the song
> of his desolation

Ungaretti's parents and ancestors were from Lucca, in Tuscany. His father had been drawn to Alexandria by Ismail Pasha's government's demand for foreigners to come and work in public works projects like the Suez Canal. Ungaretti's father died from an illness contracted while at work on excavations in the canal when Giuseppe was two years old. His mother raised him and his older brother with her earnings from the bakery she owned in an Italian section of Alexandria. Alexandria and the desert next to which Ungaretti lived, as well as the Bedouin culture he witnessed there, became huge, timeless images in the poet's imagination. For Ungaretti, the desert was the aptest of images for the eternity in which our lives are the mirages. He was ambivalent about the desert and the city that borders it. At times they are places of Edenic bliss:

> Now
> the clear sky
> is closed
> like the jasmine
> at this hour
> in my native Africa

At other times they are places of delusion and madness:

If the Arab returns from the desert, ah! mastiffs are barking in his veins. This is why the nomad is incurable: the desert is a wine, and it is a drug, and it sets a rage on fire that can be quenched only in blood and in languorous loves.

Out of the many senses of death that his thousands-of-years existence has impressed in his veins, the Egyptian has received the saddest sense from the Arab: that the desire for pleasure is a radical thirst, suffering that does not ease up except in madness. This sense: that madness is like an increase of soul, that the soul's prize is liberation into the mortal pleasure of the senses.

As Ungaretti put it in his 1965 interview: "The image of desolation has been an obsession for me since my first poems. To be precise, the desert was in me: from it was born ... the motion and the feeling of infinity, of the primordial, of the decline into nothingness." Thus the desert represented for him both the fullness and the emptiness of eternity; and Alexandria, the city on the desert, was a symbol for the ephemerality of civilization itself. The austerity of Ungaretti's spirituality—his negative theology—had much in common with that of the Desert Fathers, the ancient monks in the desert near Alexandria. Ungaretti was strongly inclined toward Platonism (as was Bergson), but he was also a skeptic. In contrast to Blake, whom he admired and translated, and in contrast to Dante as well, Ungaretti did not ultimately trust that products of the imagination were anything other than mirages—he was more Jansenist than Kabbalist. Hence his obsession with the Baroque and its "multiplication of units" to fill in "the void," the fear of emptiness that he said motivated its frantic attempt to fill up the empty spaces:

When one is in the presence of the Colosseum, an enormous cylinder with empty eye sockets, one has the sense of emptiness. Naturally, having the sense of emptiness, one cannot help but also have the dread of emptiness. Those things piled up, coming from every direction, so that not a bit of space is left, of free space, everything is filled, nothing is left, nothing freed. That dread of emptiness, one can feel it in Rome infinitely more than in any other place on earth, more even than in the desert. I believe that from the dread of emptiness issues, not the need of filling that space with it-matters-not-what-thing, but all the drama of the art of Michelangelo.

When I said that the Baroque provoked the sense of emptiness, that the aesthetic of the Roman Baroque had been initiated by the dread of emptiness, I mentioned the Colosseum. I'm afraid I haven't been clear enough. The dread in the Baroque originated with the intolerable idea of a body without a soul. A skeleton evokes the dread of emptiness.

For Ungaretti, poetry is a means for using memory, the collective memory that language embodies, to rediscover innocence, "the world resurrected in its native purity." A challenge in Ungaretti's time and ours is to reinterpret the present in relation to a disintegrated past. Ungaretti rejected the Futurists' pretense that the rubble of the past could simply be swept aside, while also affirming Leopardi's despairing realization that an age was spent. As Ungaretti put it in an essay four years before his death in 1970:

After the war we witnessed a change in the world that separated us from what we used to be and from what we once had made and done, as if at one blow millions of years had passed. Things grew old, fit only for a museum. Today everything that is stored in books is listened to as a testimony of the past, not as our own mode of expression . . . Something in the world of languages is totally finished . . . We are men cut off from our own depths.

Modern (or postmodern) man, he said, is "trapped in the impossibility of speech, in the violence stronger than the word." It is remarkable that Ungaretti, like his master Leopardi, expressed such torment so beautifully, giving us a language for where we are in relation to what we have lost.

GIUSEPPE UNGARETTI SELECTED POEMS

FROM L'allegria

Eterno

Tra un fiore colto e l'altro donato
l'inesprimibile nulla

Between one flower plucked and the other given
the inexpressible nothing

Levante

.

La linea
vaporosa muore
al lontano cerchio del cielo

Picchi di tacchi picchi di mani
e il clarino ghirigori striduli
e il mare è cenerino
trema dolce inquieto
come un piccione

A poppa emigranti soriani ballano

A prua un giovane è solo

Di sabato sera a quest'ora
Ebrei
laggiù
portano via
i loro morti
nell'imbuto di chiocciola
tentennamenti
di vicoli
di lumi

Confusa acqua
come il chiasso di poppa che odo
dentro l'ombra
del
sonno

The puffy line
dies
in the distant circle of sky

Tip-tops of heels tip-tops of hands
and shrieking doodles of clarinet
and the ocean is ashen
trembles tender agitated
as a pigeon

Syrian emigrants dance astern

A young man is alone at the bow

On Saturday evening at this hour
Jews
down there
carry away
their dead
on the snail-shell-funnel
waverings
of narrow lanes
of lamps

Jumbled water
like the uproar at the stern I hear
inside
the shadow
of sleep

Agonia

Morire come le allodole assetate
sul miraggio

O come la quaglia
passato il mare
nei primi cespugli
perché di volare
non ha più voglia

Ma non vivere di lamento
come un cardellino accecato

Agony

To die like skylarks thirsty
over the mirage

Or like the quail
after crossing the sea
inside the first bushes
because it has no wish
to fly anymore

But not to live lamenting
like a goldfinch blinded

Notte di maggio

Il cielo pone in capo
ai minareti
ghirlande di lumini

May Night

The sky arranges garlands
of votive candles
on the tops of minarets

In memoria

Locvizza il 30 settembre 1916

Si chiamava
Moammed Sceab

Discendente
di emiri di nomadi
suicida
perché non aveva più
Patria

Amò la Francia
e mutò nome

Fu Marcel
ma non era Francese
e non sapeva più
vivere
nella tenda dei suoi
dove si ascolta la cantilena
del Corano
gustando un caffè

E non sapeva
sciogliere
il canto
del suo abbandono

L'ho accompagnato
insieme alla padrona dell'albergo

In Memory Of

Locvizza, September 30, 1916

His name was
Mohammed Sceab

Descendant
of emirs of nomads
a suicide
because he had no homeland
left

He loved France
and changed his name

He was Marcel
but wasn't French
and no longer knew
how to live
in his people's tent
where you hear the Koran
being chanted
while you savor your coffee

And he didn't know how
to set free
the song
of his desolation

I went with him
and the proprietress of the hotel

dove abitavamo
a Parigi
dal numero 5 della Rue des Carmes
appassito vicolo in discesa

Riposa
nel camposanto d'Ivry
sobborgo che pare
sempre
in una giornata
di una decomposta fiera

E forse io solo
so ancora
che visse

where we lived
in Paris
from number 5 Rue des Carmes
an old faded alley sloping downhill

He rests
in the graveyard at Ivry
a suburb that always
seems
like the day
a fair breaks down

And perhaps only I
still know
he lived

Il porto sepolto

Mariano il 29 giugno 1916

Vi arriva il poeta
e poi torna alla luce con i suoi canti
e li disperde

Di questa poesia
mi resta
quel nulla
d'inesauribile segreto

The Buried Harbor

Mariano, June 29, 1916

The poet arrives there
and then resurfaces with his songs
and scatters them

All that's left me
of this—this poetry:
the merest nothing
of an inexhaustible secret

Veglia

Cima Quattro il 23 dicembre 1915

Un'intera nottata
buttato vicino
a un compagno
massacrato
con la sua bocca
digrignata
volta al plenilunio
con la congestione
delle sue mani
penetrata
nel mio silenzio
ho scritto
lettere piene d'amore

Non sono mai stato
tanto
attaccato alla vita

Vigil

Cima Quattro, December 23, 1915

An entire night
thrown down
beside a
butchered
companion with his
grimacing
mouth turned
to the full moon
with his congested hands
thrust
into my silence
I wrote
letters full of love

I have never held
so hard
to life

A riposo

Versa il 27 aprile 1916

Chi mi accompagnerà pei campi

Il sole si semina in diamanti
di gocciole d'acqua
sull'erba flessuosa

Resto docile
all'inclinazione
dell'universo sereno

Si dilatano le montagne
in sorsi d'ombra lilla
e vogano col cielo

Su alla volta lieve
l'incanto s'è troncato

E piombo in me

E m'oscuro in un mio nido

Resting

Versa, April 27, 1916

Who will come with me through the fields

The sunlight is scattered in diamond
drops of water
over the supple grass

I am surrendered
to the leanings
of the limpid universe

The mountains open out
in deep draughts of lilac shadow
and row with the sky

Up in the light vault
the spell is broken

And I plummet into myself

And go dark in my nest

Tramonto

Versa il 20 maggio 1916

Il carnato del cielo
sveglia oasi
al nomade d'amore

Sunset

Versa, May 20, 1916

The flesh-pink of the sky
awakens oases
in the nomad of love

Dannazione

Mariano il 29 giugno 1916

Chiuso fra cose mortali

(Anche il cielo stellato finirà)

Perché bramo Dio?

Damnation

Mariano, June 29, 1916

Closed off among things that die

(Even the starry sky will end)

Why do I long for God?

Risvegli

Mariano il 29 giugno 1916

Ogni mio momento
io l'ho vissuto
un'altra volta
in un'epoca fonda
fuori di me

Sono lontano colla mia memoria
dietro a quelle vite perse

Mi desto in un bagno
di care cose consuete
sorpreso
e raddolcito

Rincorro le nuvole
che si sciolgono dolcemente
cogli occhi attenti
e mi rammento
di qualche amico
morto

Ma Dio cos'è?

E la creatura
atterrita
sbarra gli occhi

Reawakenings

Mariano, June 29, 1916

My every moment
I've lived
another time
in a deep period
outside me

I'm a long way off with my memory
behind those lost lives

I wake
awash in dear everyday things
surprised
and comforted

With vigilant eyes
I chase the clouds
that gently dissolve
and remember
a few dead
friends

But what is God?

And the terrified
creature
opens wide his eyes

e accoglie
gocciole di stelle
e la pianura muta

E si sente
riavere

and welcomes
stardrops
and the silent plain

And feels
himself again

Fratelli

Mariano il 15 luglio 1916

Di che reggimento siete
fratelli?

Parola tremante
nella notte

Foglia appena nata

Nell'aria spasimante
involontaria rivolta
dell'uomo presente alla sua
fragilità

Fratelli

Brothers

Mariano, July 15, 1916

What regiment are you from
brothers?

Word shuddering
in the night

Leaf barely open

In the anguishing air
involuntary rebellion
of man present to his own
frailness

Brothers

C'era una volta

Quota Centoquarantuno l'1 agosto 1916

Bosco Cappuccio
ha un declivio
di velluto verde
come una dolce
poltrona

Appisolarmi là
solo
in un caffè remoto
con una luce fievole
come questa
di questa luna

Once upon a Time

Quota Centoquarantuno, August 1, 1916

In Cappuccio Forest
there's a slope
of green velvet
like a lovely
overstuffed chair

My dozing off there
alone
in a far-off café
with a faint light
like this one
this moon is shedding

I fiumi

Cotici il 16 agosto 1916

Mi tengo a quest'albero mutilato
abbandonato in questa dolina
che ha il languore
di un circo
prima o dopo lo spettacolo
e guardo
il passaggio quieto
delle nuvole sulla luna

Stamani mi sono disteso
in un'urna d'acqua
e come una reliquia
ho riposato

L'Isonzo scorrendo
mi levigava
come un suo sasso

Ho tirato su
le mie quattr'ossa
e me ne sono andato
come un acrobata
sull'acqua

Mi sono accoccolato
vicino ai miei panni
sudici di guerra

The Rivers

Cotici, August 16, 1916

I hang on to this mangled tree
abandoned in this sinkhole
that is listless
as a circus
before or after the show
and watch
the quiet passage
of clouds across the moon

This morning I stretched out
in an urn of water
and rested
like a relic

The flowing Isonzo
smoothed me
like one of its stones

I hoisted up
my sack of bones
and got out of there
like an acrobat
over the water

I crouched
beside my grimy
battle clothes

e come un beduino
mi sono chinato a ricevere
il sole

Questo è l'Isonzo
e qui meglio
mi sono riconosciuto
una docile fibra
dell'universo

Il mio supplizio
è quando
non mi credo
in armonia

Ma quelle occulte
mani
che m'intridono
mi regalano
la rara
felicità

Ho ripassato
le epoche
della mia vita

Questi sono
i miei fiumi

Questo è il Serchio
al quale hanno attinto
duemil'anni forse

and like a Bedouin
bent to greet
the sun

This is the Isonzo
and here I recognized myself
more clearly
as a pliant fiber
of the universe

My affliction
is when
I don't believe myself
in harmony

But those hidden
hands
that knead me
freely give
the uncommon
bliss

I went back over
the ages
of my life

These are
my rivers

This is the Serchio
where maybe
two millennia of my farming people

di gente mia campagnola
e mio padre e mia madre

Questo è il Nilo
che mi ha visto
nascere e crescere
e ardere d'inconsapevolezza
nelle estese pianure

Questa è la Senna
e in quel suo torbido
mi sono rimescolato
e mi sono conosciuto

Questi sono i miei fiumi
contati nell'Isonzo

Questa è la mia nostalgia
che in ognuno
mi traspare
ora ch'è notte
che la mia vita mi pare
una corolla
di tenebre

and my father and mother
drew their water

This is the Nile
that saw me
born and raised
and burn with unawareness
on the sweeping flatlands

This is the Seine
within whose roiling waters
I was mixed again
and came to know myself

These are my rivers
reckoned in the Isonzo

This is my longing for home
that in each one
shines through me
now that it's night
that my life seems
a corolla
of darkness

Pellegrinaggio

Valloncello dell'Albero Isolato il 16 agosto 1916

In agguato
in queste budella
di macerie
ore e ore
ho strascicato
la mia carcassa
usata dal fango
come una suola
o come un seme
di spinalba

Ungaretti
uomo di pena
ti basta un'illusione
per farti coraggio

Un riflettore
di là
mette un mare
nella nebbia

Pilgrimage

Gully of the Isolated Tree, August 16, 1916

Trapped
inside these bowels
of rubble
hours and hours
I dragged
my carcass
worn down by mud
like a shoe sole
or like a seed
of white thorn

Ungaretti
man of pain
all you need is an illusion
to give you courage

A searchlight
over there
creates an ocean
in the fog

Monotonia

Valloncello dell'Albero Isolato il 22 agosto 1916

Fermato a due sassi
languisco
sotto questa
volta appannata
di cielo

Il groviglio dei sentieri
possiede la mia cecità

Nulla è più squallido
di questa monotonia

Una volta
non sapevo
ch'è una cosa
qualunque
perfino
la consunzione serale
del cielo

E sulla mia terra affricana
calmata
a un arpeggio
perso nell'aria
mi rinnovavo

Monotony

Gully of the Isolated Tree, August 22, 1916

Halted at two boulders
I am languishing
under this
dimmed vault
of sky

The maze of paths
possesses my blindness

Nothing's more dismal
than this unending sameness

Once
I did not know
that even
the sky's
annihilation at evening
is just
an ordinary thing

And on my lulled
African soil
I was brought back to life
by an arpeggio
drifting in the air

La notte bella

Devetachi il 24 agosto 1916

Quale canto s'è levato stanotte
che intesse
di cristallina eco del cuore
le stelle

Quale festa sorgiva
di cuore a nozze

Sono stato
uno stagno di buio

Ora mordo
come un bambino la mammella
lo spazio

Ora sono ubriaco
d'universo

Beautiful Night

Devetachi, August 24, 1916

What song has risen tonight
that weaves
the crystal echo of the heart
with stars

What green banquet
of the marrying heart

I was a standing
pool of darkness

Now I bite
space
like a baby his mother's breast

Now I am drunk
on vastness

San Martino del Carso

Valloncello dell'Albero Isolato il 27 agosto 1916

Di queste case
non è rimasto
che qualche
brandello di muro

Di tanti
che mi corrispondevano
non è rimasto
neppure tanto

Ma nel cuore
nessuna croce manca

È il mio cuore
il paese più straziato

San Martino del Carso

Gully of the Isolated Tree, August 27, 1916

Nothing is left
of these houses
but a few
tatters of wall

Out of the many people
who used to be like me
not even
that much is left

But in my heart
there is no shortage of crosses

My heart is the village
most smashed to pieces

Attrito

Locvizza il 23 settembre 1916

Con la mia fame di lupo
ammaino
il mio corpo di pecorella

Sono come
la misera barca
e come l'oceano libidinoso

Friction

Locvizza, September 23, 1916

With my wolf's hunger
I haul my lamb's body
down like a sail

I am like
the wretched boat
and the lascivious sea

Italia

Locvizza l'1 ottobre 1916

Sono un poeta
un grido unanime
sono un grumo di sogni

Sono un frutto
d'innumerevoli contrasti d'innesti
maturato in una serra

Ma il tuo popolo è portato
dalla stessa terra
che mi porta
Italia

E in questa uniforme
di tuo soldato
mi riposo
come fosse la culla
di mio padre

Italy

I am a poet
a unanimous outcry
I am a clot of dreams

I am a fruit
of countless contrasting grafts
matured in a hothouse

But your people
Italy
sprang from the same earth
I sprang from

And in this your
soldier's uniform
I am at peace
as if it were my father's
cradle

Commiato

Locvizza il 2 ottobre 1916

Gentile
Ettore Serra
poesia
è il mondo l'umanità
la propria vita
fioriti dalla parola
la limpida meraviglia
di un delirante fermento

Quando trovo
in questo mio silenzio
una parola
scavata è nella mia vita
come un abisso

Envoi

Locvizza, October 2, 1916

Dear
Ettore Serra
poetry
is world humanity
one's very life
blossomed from the word
the limpid marvel
of a raving ferment

When I find
a word
in this my silence
it is dug into my life
like an abyss

Allegria di naufragi

Versa il 14 febbraio 1917

E subito riprende
il viaggio
come
dopo il naufragio
un superstite
lupo di mare

Joy of Shipwrecks

Versa, February 14, 1917

And promptly takes up
the voyage again
like
a sea wolf
who has survived
the shipwreck

Un'altra notte

Vallone il 20 aprile 1917

In quest'oscuro
colle mani
gelate
distinguo
il mio viso

Mi vedo
abbandonato nell'infinito

Another Night

Vallone, April 20, 1917

In this darkness
with frozen
hands
I make out
my face

I see myself
deserted in boundlessness

Giugno

Campolongo il 5 luglio 1917

Quando
mi morirà
questa notte
e come un altro
potrò guardarla
e mi addormenterò
al fruscio
delle onde
che finiscono
di avvoltolarsi
alla cinta di gaggie
della mia casa

Quando mi risveglierò
nel tuo corpo
che si modula
come la voce dell'usignolo

Si estenua
come il colore
rilucente
del grano
maturo

Nella trasparenza
dell'acqua
l'oro velino

June

Campolongo, July 5, 1917

When
will this night
die
so that I
can look at it
like another man
and fall asleep
to the swash
of waves that finish
their coiling
at the wall of black locusts
outside my house

When will I wake again
in your body
that varies its tones
like the call of the nightingale

It fades
like the luminous
color
of ripened
wheat

In the water's
transparence
the golden tissue

della tua pelle
si brinerà di moro

Librata
dalle lastre
squillanti
dell'aria sarai
come una
pantera

Ai tagli
mobili
dell'ombra
ti sfoglierai

Ruggendo
muta in
quella polvere
mi soffocherai

Poi
socchiuderai le palpebre

Vedremo il nostro amore reclinarsi
come sera

Poi vedrò
rasserenato
nell'orizzonte di bitume
delle tue iridi morirmi
le pupille

of your skin
will be frosted brown

You'll be
like a
panther
balanced
on the shrill
panels of air

At the moving
edges
of shadow
you'll shed your leaves

Roaring
mute within
that dust
you'll smother me

Then
you'll half close your eyes

We'll see our love lie down
like evening

Then at peace again
I'll see
my pupils die
on the bitumen horizon
of your irises

Ora
il sereno è chiuso
come
a quest'ora
nel mio paese d'Affrica
i gelsumini

Ho perso il sonno

Oscillo
al canto d'una strada
come una lucciola

Mi morirà
questa notte?

Now
the clear sky
is closed
like the jasmine
at this hour
in my native Africa

Sleep eludes me

I waver
at the corner of a road
like a firefly

Will this night
die in me?

Vanità

Vallone il 19 agosto 1917

D'improvviso
è alto
sulle macerie
il limpido
stupore
dell'immensità

E l'uomo
curvato
sull'acqua
sorpresa
dal sole
si rinviene
un'ombra

Cullata e
piano
franta

Vanity

Vallone, August 19, 1917

Suddenly
the lucid
awesome
vastness
is high
above the rubble

And the man
bent
over the sun-
shocked
water
finds
he's a shadow

Rocked and
gently
broken

Girovago

Campo di Mailly maggio 1918

In nessuna
parte
di terra
mi posso
accasare

A ogni
nuovo
clima
che incontro
mi trovo
languente
che
una volta
già gli ero stato
assuefatto

E me ne stacco sempre
straniero

Nascendo
tornato da epoche troppo
vissute

Godere un solo
minuto di vita
iniziale

Cerco un paese
innocente

Wanderer

Campo di Mailly, May 1918

There is no
place
on earth
where I
can settle down

In every
new
climate
I come upon
I find myself
languishing
because
once I'd already
got used
to it

And I always pull myself away
a stranger

Being born
back again from periods much
too lived

To delight in just
one minute of inchoate
life

I am seeking an innocent
country

Lucca

A casa mia, in Egitto, dopo cena, recitato il rosario, mia madre ci parlava di questi posti.

La mia infanzia ne fu tutta meraviglia.

La città ha un traffico timorato e fanatico.

In queste mura non ci si sta che di passaggio.

Qui la meta è partire.

Mi sono seduto al fresco sulla porta dell'osteria con della gente che mi parla di California come d'un suo podere.

Mi scopro con terrore nei connotati di queste persone.

Ora lo sento scorrere caldo nelle mie vene, il sangue dei miei morti.

Ho preso anch'io una zappa.

Nelle cosce fumanti della terra mi scopro a ridere.

Addio desideri, nostalgie.

So di passato e d'avvenire quanto un uomo può saperne.

Conosco ormai il mio destino, e la mia origine.

Non mi rimane più nulla da profanare, nulla da sognare.

Ho goduto di tutto, e sofferto.

Non mi rimane che rassegnarmi a morire.

Alleverò dunque tranquillamente una prole.

Quando un appetito maligno mi spingeva negli amori mortali, lodavo la vita.

Ora che considero, *anch'io*, l'amore come una garanzia della specie, ho in vista la morte.

At my house in Egypt, after supper and reciting the rosary, my
mother used to tell us about these places.

My childhood was all amazement over them.

The goings-on in this town are scrupulous and fanatical.

No one enters these walls except in passing.

The main aim here is to leave.

I sit outside the entrance to the tavern with some people who
tell me about California like it's one of their farms.

I'm terrified as I discover myself in their features.

Now I feel it running hot in my veins, the blood of
my dead.

I too have held a hoe.

In the steaming thighs of the earth I find myself laughing.

Farewell, desires, nostalgias.

I know as much about the past and future as a man is able.

I already know my fate and origin.

There's nothing left for me to defile, nothing to dream about.

I've enjoyed everything, and endured.

There's nothing left for me but to resign myself to dying.

Peacefully, therefore, I shall raise an offspring.

When a malicious hunger drove me into mortal loves,
I praised life.

Now that I—*even I*—think of love as a guarantee of the
species, I have death in sight.

FROM # A Sense of Time

O notte

1919

Dall'ampia ansia dell'alba
Svelata alberatura.

Dolorosi risvegli.

Foglie, sorelle foglie,
Vi ascolto nel lamento.

Autunni,
Moribonde dolcezze.

O gioventù,
Passata è appena l'ora del distacco.

Cieli alti della gioventù,
Libero slancio.

E già sono deserto.

Perso in questa curva malinconia.

Ma la notte sperde le lontananze.

Oceanici silenzi,
Astrali nidi d'illusione,

O notte.

O Night

Out of daybreak's huge and restless hunger
Trees—like masts—revealed.

Anguished awakenings.

Leaves, sister leaves,
I hear your lament.

Autumns,
Dying sweetnesses.

O youth,
Only just past now, the moment of detachment.

Towering skies of youth,
Unbridled surge.

And already I am desert.

Lost inside this curving sadness.

But night disperses distances.

Oceanic silences,
Astral nests of wishes,

O night.

Silenzio in Liguria

Scade flessuosa la pianura d'acqua.

Nelle sue urne il sole
Ancora segreto si bagna.

Una carnagione lieve trascorre.

Ed ella apre improvvisa ai seni
La grande mitezza degli occhi.

L'ombra sommersa delle rocce muore.

Dolce sbocciata dalle anche ilari,
Il vero amore è una quiete accesa,

E la godo diffusa
Dall'ala alabastrina
D'una mattina immobile.

Silence in Liguria

1922

The supple plain of water dwindles.

Within its urns the sun
Bathes, secret again.

A delicate complexion flits by.

And she opens without forethought toward the bays
The immense mildness of her eyes.

The sunken shadow of the rocks expires.

Sweet blossomed from blithe hips,
The true love is a burning stillness,

And I enjoy it fanned
Out from the alabaster wing
Of a motionless morning.

Sirene

1923

Funesto spirito
Che accendi e turbi amore,
Affine io torni senza requie all'alto
Con impazienza le apparenze muti,
E già, prima ch'io giunga a qualche meta,
Non ancora deluso
M'avvinci ad altro sogno.
Uguale a un mare che irrequieto e blando
Da lungi porga e celi
Un'isola fatale,
Con varietà d'inganni
Accompagni chi non dispera, a morte.

Deadly spirit
Who kindles and unsettles love,
That I may keep returning to high seas,
Unable to stay still, you change appearances,
And already, before I reach some goal,
Illusions intact,
You snare me with another dream.
Just as a sea that restless and mild
From far off shows and conceals
A fateful island,
With various deceptions
You usher him who doesn't despair, to death.

Ricordo d'Affrica

1924

Non più ora tra la piana sterminata
E il largo mare m'apparterò, né umili
Di remote età, udrò più sciogliersi, chiari,
Nell'aria limpida, squilli; né più
Le grazie acerbe andrà nudando
E in forme favolose esalterà
Folle la fantasia,
Né dal rado palmeto Diana apparsa
In agile abito di luce,
Rincorreró
(In un suo gelo altiera s'abbagliava,
Ma le seguiva gli occhi nel posarli
Arroventando disgraziate brame,
Per sempre
Infinito velluto).

È solo linea vaporosa il mare
Che un giorno germogliò rapace,
E nappo d'un miele, non più gustato
Per non morire di sete, mi pare
La piana, e a un seno casto, Diana vezzo
D'opali, ma nemmeno d'invisibile
Non palpita.

Ah! questa è l'ora che annuvola e smemora.

Memory of Africa

1924

No more now will I go off alone
Between the vast plain and the open sea,
Nor hear, from far-off ages, homely, clear,
Loosening in the limpid air, shrill sounds;
Nor will crazy fantasy go stripping nude
The acid graces,
Exalting them in fabled forms;
Nor will I pursue Diana
Stepping from the sparse palm grove
In a fleet gown of light
(In her haughtiness and ice she dazzled,
But wherever her eyes rested,
Burning red hot wretched want, followed
Forever
Infinite velvet).

The sea is only a vaporous line
That once budded devouring, and the plain
Looks like a cup of honey
No longer savored, so as not to die
Of thirst, and at a chaste breast, Diana string
Of opals, but it doesn't pulsate
Even with the invisible.

Ah! this is the hour that clouds and fades remembering.

L'isola

1925

A una proda ove sera era perenne
Di anziane selve assorte, scese,
E s'inoltrò
E lo richiamò rumore di penne
Ch'erasi sciolto dallo stridulo
Batticuore dell'acqua torrida,
E una larva (languiva
E rifioriva) vide;
Ritornato a salire vide
Ch'era una ninfa e dormiva
Ritta abbracciata a un olmo.

In sé da simulacro a fiamma vera
Errando, giunse a un prato ove
L'ombra negli occhi s'addensava
Delle vergini come
Sera appiè degli ulivi;
Distillavano i rami
Una pioggia pigra di dardi,
Qua pecore s'erano appisolate
Sotto il liscio tepore,
Altre brucavano
La coltre luminosa;
Le mani del pastore erano un vetro
Levigato da fioca febbre.

The Island

1925

He landed on a waterfront where evening
Was everlasting, thick with ancient spellbound trees,
And made his way in,
And a flutter of feathers
Loosened from the piercing palpitations
Of the scalding water
Called him back, and he thought he saw
(Fading, reflourishing)
A shade; climbing again,
He saw it was a nymph
Asleep on her feet, her arms around an elm.

Roaming around inside himself from imitation
To the true flame, he reached a meadow
Where the shadow in the eyes
Of virgins thickened like evening
In a grove of olives;
The branches dripped
A lazy rain of arrows;
A few sheep drowzed
Beneath the tepid glaze,
Others nibbled
The luminous blanket;
The shepherd's hands were glass
Polished by mild fever.

Lago luna alba notte

1927

Gracili arbusti, ciglia
Di celato bisbiglio...

Impallidito livore rovina...

Un uomo, solo, passa
Col suo sgomento muto...

Conca lucente,
Trasporti alla foce del sole!

Torni ricolma di riflessi, anima,
E ritrovi ridente
L'oscuro...

Tempo, fuggitivo tremito...

Lake Moon Dawn Night

1927

Delicate bushes, cilia
Of concealed whispers . . .

Malice gone pale collapses . . .

A man passes alone
With his silent dread . . .

Shining basin,
Transport to the mouth of the sun!

You return resplendent with reflections, soul,
Laughing you retrieve
The dark . . .

Time, fleeting tremor . . .

Inno alla morte

1925

Amore, mio giovine emblema,
Tornato a dorare la terra,
Diffuso entro il giorno rupestre,
È l'ultima volta che miro
(Appiè del botro, d'irruenti
Acque sontuoso, d'antri
Funesto) la scia di luce
Che pari alla tortora lamentosa
Sull'erba svagata si turba.

Amore, salute lucente,
Mi pesano gli anni venturi.

Abbandonata la mazza fedele,
Scivolerò nell'acqua buia
Senza rimpianto.

Morte, arido fiume . . .

Immemore sorella, morte,
L'uguale mi farai del sogno
Baciandomi.

Avrò il tuo passo,
Andrò senza lasciare impronta.

Hymn to Death

1925

Love, my youthful emblem,
Returned to gild the earth,
Diffused inside the craggy day,
This is the last time I'll gaze
(At the foot of the ravine, lush
With streaming waters, bleak
With caverns) on your track of light
Which like the desolate dove
Distracted on the grass grows dim.

Love, radiant health,
The years to come are heavy weight.

My trusty walking stick abandoned,
I'll slip into the dark water
Without regret.

Death, desiccated river . . .

Unremembering sister, death,
Kissing me
You'll make me the peer of dream.

I'll have your way of walking,
I'll leave no trace.

Mi darai il cuore immobile
D'un iddio, sarò innocente,
Non avrò più pensieri né bontà.

Colla mente murata,
Cogli occhi caduti in oblio,
Farò da guida alla felicità.

You'll instill in me a god's
Unmoving heart, I'll be innocent—
No more thoughts or goodness.

With my memory walled up,
Eyes fallen in oblivion,
I'll become a guide to bliss.

Di luglio

1931

Quando su ci si butta lei,
Si fa d'un triste colore di rosa
Il bel fogliame.

Strugge forre, beve fiumi,
Macina scogli, splende,
È furia che s'ostina, è implacabile,
Sparge spazio, acceca mete,
È l'estate e nei secoli
Con i suoi occhi calcinanti
Va della terra spogliando lo scheletro.

In July

1931

When she hurls herself at it headlong,
The lovely foliage
Turns a sad shade of rose.

She liquifies ravines, drinks rivers,
Crushes crags, shines,
She's fury that won't let up, she's unappeasable,
She scatters space, blinds purpose,
She's summer and over centuries
With her calcining eyes
She goes about stripping the earth's skeleton.

Giunone

1931

Tonda quel tanto che mi dà tormento,
La tua coscia distacca di sull'altra . . .

Dilati la tua furia un'acre notte!

Juno

1931

So round and full it drives me mad,
One of your thighs pulls away from the other . . .

May your frenzy open wide an acrid night!

D'agosto

1925

Avido lutto ronzante nei vivi,

Monotono altomare,
Ma senza solitudine,

Repressi squilli da prostrate messi,

Estate,

Sino ad orbite ombrate spolpi selci,

Risvegli ceneri nei colossei . . .

Quale Erebo t'urlò?

In August

Voracious mourning buzzing in the living,

Monotonous high sea,
Minus the solitude,

Stifled squeals from prostrate fields of grain,

Summer,

You flay flagstones into shadowy eye sockets,

Reawaken ashes in colosseums . . .

What Erebus howled you?

Ogni grigio

1925

Dalla spoglia di serpe
Alla pavida talpa
Ogni grigio si gingilla sui duomi ...

Come una prora bionda
Di stella in stella il sole s'accomiata
E s'acciglia sotto la pergola ...

Come una fronte stanca
È riapparsa la notte
Nel cavo d'una mano ...

Every Gray

1925

From serpent's slough
To fearful mole
Every gray dawdles on the cathedrals ...

Like a golden prow
From star to star the sun takes leave
And frowns beneath the arbor ...

Like a weary brow,
Night has reappeared
In the hollow of a hand ...

Fine di Crono

1925

L'ora impaurita
In grembo al firmamento
Erra strana.

Una fuligine
Lilla corona i monti,

Fu l'ultimo grido a smarrirsi.

Penelopi innumeri, astri

Vi riabbraccia il Signore!

(Ah, cecità!
Frana delle notti . . .)

E riporge l'Olimpo,
Fiore eterno di sonno.

End of Chronos

1925

The strange and frightened moment
Wanders in the lap
Of the firmament.

A lilac-tinted smudge
Crowns the mountains,

The last outcry to stray.

Countless Penelopes, stars

The Lord embraces you again!

(Ah, blindness!
Cave-in of nights ...)

And offers back Olympus,
Eternal flower of sleep.

Con fuoco

1925

Con fuoco d'occhi un nostalgico lupo
Scorre la quiete nuda.

Non trova che ombre di cielo sul ghiaccio,

Fondono serpi fatue e brevi viole.

With Fire

1925

With fire in his eyes a homesick wolf
Scours the naked quiet.

All he finds are shadows of sky on the ice,

Blending evanescent serpents and flickering violets.

Ultimo quarto

1927

Luna,
Piuma di cielo,
Così velina,
Arida,
Trasporti il murmure d'anime spoglie?

E alla pallida che diranno mai
Pipistrelli dai ruderi del teatro,
In sogno quelle capre,
E fra arse foglie come in fermo fumo
Con tutto il suo sgolarsi di cristallo
Un usignuolo?

Last Quarter

Moon,
Feather of heaven,
Such onionskin,
Barren,
Do you convey the murmur of souls laid bare?

And what will they ever say to the pale one,
Bats from the theater ruins,
Those goats in dream,
And among burnt foliage as in hanging smoke
With all its crystal singing-out-its-throat
A nightingale?

Statua

1927

Gioventù impietrita,
O statua, o statua dell'abisso umano . . .

Il gran tumulto dopo tanto viaggio
Corrode uno scoglio
A fiore di labbra.

Statue

1927

Petrified youth,
O statue, O statue of the human abyss . . .

After so much journeying the great tumult
Wears down a reef
In whispers.

Stelle

1927

Tornano in alto ad ardere le favole.

Cadranno colle foglie al primo vento.

Ma venga un altro soffio,
Ritornerà scintillamento nuovo.

Stars

1927

The fables are in flames again up high.

They'll fall with leaves at the first wind.

But let there be another breath of air,
Glistening will return anew.

Grido

1928

Giunta la sera,
Riposavo sopra l'erba monotona,
E presi gusto
A quella brama senza fine,
Grido torbido e alato
Che la luce quando muore trattiene.

Outcry

1928

Evening having arrived,
I rested on the monotonous grass
And savored
That perpetual desire,
Dark and flying outcry,
Which the light when it dies holds back.

Quiete

1929

L'uva è matura, il campo arato,

Si stacca il monte dalle nuvole.

Sui polverosi specchi dell'estate
Caduta è l'ombra,

Tra le dita incerte
Il loro lume è chiaro,
E lontano.

Colle rondini fugge
L'ultimo strazio.

Stillness

1929

The grapes are heavy, the field plowed,

The mountain is withdrawing from the clouds.

The shadow has fallen
Over summer's dusty mirrors,

Between faltering fingers
Their shine is clear,
And distant.

With the swallows flees
The final torment.

Sera

1929

Appiè dei passi della sera
Va un'acqua chiara
Colore dell'uliva,

E giunge al breve fuoco smemorato.

Nel fumo ora odo grilli e rane,

Dove tenere tremano erbe.

Evening

1929

At the foot of evening's passage
Flows a limpid
Olive-colored stream

That merges with the flickering forgetful fire.

In the smoke now I hear frogs and crickets,

Where tender grasses tremble.

Il capitano

1929

Fui pronto a tutte le partenze.

Quando hai segreti, notte hai pietà.

Se bimbo mi svegliavo
Di soprassalto, mi calmavo udendo
Urlanti nell'assente via,
Cani randagi. Mi parevano
Più del lumino alla Madonna
Che ardeva sempre in quella stanza,
Mistica compagnia.

E non ad un rincorrere
Echi d'innanzi nascita,
Mi sorpresi con cuore, uomo?

Ma quando, notte, il tuo viso fu nudo
E buttato sul sasso
Non fui che fibra d'elementi,
Pazza, palese in ogni oggetto,
Era schiacciante l'umiltà.

Il Capitano era sereno.

(Venne in cielo la luna)

Era alto e mai non si chinava.

The Captain

1929

I was always ready for departures.

When you have secrets, night, you're merciful.

When as a child I woke up
Startled, I'd soothe myself listening
To howlings in the hollow street—
Stray dogs. More than the little lamp
That burned forever in that room
Near the Madonna, they seemed
Like mystical company.

And was it not in chasing
Echoes from before my birth,
I surprised myself with heart, a man?

But when, night, your face was bare
And cast on rock
I was nothing but fiber, elemental,
Crazed, apparent in every object,
Lowliness crushed me.

The Captain was serene.

(The moon came into the sky)

He was tall and never bowed.

(Andava su una nube)

Nessuno lo vide cadere,
Nessuno l'udì rantolare,
Riapparve adagiato in un solco,
Teneva le mani sul petto.

Gli chiusi gli occhi.

(La luna è un velo)

Parve di piume.

(It climbed into a cloud)

No one saw him fall,
No one heard him gasping for air,
He reappeared laid carefully inside a furrow,
His hands were on his chest.

I closed his eyes.

(The moon is a veil)

He seemed made of feathers.

La madre

1930

E il cuore quando d'un ultimo battito
Avrà fatto cadere il muro d'ombra,
Per condurmi, Madre, sino al Signore,
Come una volta mi darai la mano.

In ginocchio, decisa,
Sarai una statua davanti all'Eterno,
Come già ti vedeva
Quando eri ancora in vita.

Alzerai tremante le vecchie braccia,
Come quando spirasti
Dicendo: Mio Dio, eccomi.

E solo quando m'avrà perdonato,
Ti verrà desiderio di guardarmi.

Ricorderai d'avermi atteso tanto,
E avrai negli occhi un rapido sospiro.

The Mother

1930

And when with a final beat my heart
Brings down the wall of shadow,
To lead me, Mother, as far as the Lord,
You'll lend me a hand as before.

You'll be on your knees, resolute,
A statue in front of the Eternal,
The way he used to see you
When you were still living.

Trembling, you'll raise your old arms,
As when you breathed your last,
Saying: Here I am, my God.

And only after he has pardoned me
Will you have the desire to look at me.

You'll remember you've waited long for my arrival,
And a rapid sighing will fill your eyes.

Dove la luce

1930

Come allodola ondosa
Nel vento lieto sui giovani prati,
Le braccia ti sanno leggera, vieni.

Ci scorderemo di quaggiù,
E del male e del cielo,
E del mio sangue rapido alla guerra,
Di passi d'ombre memori
Entro rossori di mattine nuove.

Dove non muove foglia più la luce,
Sogni e crucci passati ad altre rive,
Dov'è posata sera,
Vieni ti porterò
Alle colline d'oro.

L'ora costante, liberi d'età,
Nel suo perduto nimbo
Sarà nostro lenzuolo.

Where the Light

1930

Like a skylark on its airy way
In joyous wind over fresh meadows,
Come, my arms know you weightless.

We'll forget about down here,
And evil and heaven,
And my blood quick to battle,
And tracks of memoried shadows
In flushes of daybreaks.

Where the light no longer stirs a leaf,
Dreams and worries gone to other shores,
Where evening is set down,
Come, I'll carry you
To the golden hills.

Time stilled, free from growing old,
In its fallen nimbus
Will be our sheet.

La pietà

1928

1

Sono un uomo ferito.

E me ne vorrei andare
E finalmente giungere,
Pietà, dove si ascolta
L'uomo che è solo con sé.

Non ho che superbia e bontà.

E mi sento esiliato in mezzo agli uomini.

Ma per essi sto in pena.
Non sarei degno di tornare in me?

Ho popolato di nomi il silenzio.

Ho fatto a pezzi cuore e mente
Per cadere in servitù di parole?

Regno sopra fantasmi.

O foglie secche,
Anima portata qua e là . . .

No, odio il vento e la sua voce
Di bestia immemorabile.

Mercy

1928

1

I am a wounded man.

And I hope someday to leave
And finally arrive,
Mercy, where the solitary man
At last is heard.

I have nothing but pride and goodness.

And I feel exiled among human beings.

Yet I'm in pain for them.
Am I not worthy to find myself again?

I have peopled the silence with names.

Have I ripped mind and heart to pieces
To fall into servitude to words?

I am king of phantoms.

O dry leaves,
Soul carried here and there ...

No, I hate the wind and its beastly
Immemorial voice.

Dio, coloro che t'implorano
Non ti conoscono più che di nome?

M'hai discacciato dalla vita.

Mi discaccerai dalla morte?

Forse l'uomo è anche indegno di sperare.

Anche la fonte del rimorso è secca?

Il peccato che importa,
Se alla purezza non conduce più.

La carne si ricorda appena
Che una volta fu forte.

È folle e usata, l'anima.

Dio, guarda la nostra debolezza.

Vorremmo una certezza.

Di noi nemmeno più ridi?

E compiangici dunque, crudeltà.

Non ne posso più di stare murato
Nel desiderio senza amore.

Una traccia mostrarci di giustizia.

God, do those who call on you now
Know you only by name?

You have cut me off from life.

Will you cut me off from death?

Maybe man doesn't even deserve to hope.

Has even the well-spring of regret gone dry?

What difference does sin make
If it no longer leads to purity?

The flesh can scarcely recollect
A time when it was strong.

The soul is used and foolish.

God, consider our frailty.

We would like a certainty.

Do you not even mock us anymore?

Well then, pity us, cruelty.

I can no longer stay walled off
In longing without love.

Show us some sign of justice.

La tua legge qual è?

Fulmina le mie povere emozioni,
Liberami dall'inquietudine.

Sono stanco di urlare senza voce.

2

Malinconiosa carne
Dove una volta pullulò la gioia,
Occhi socchiusi del risveglio stanco,
Tu vedi, anima troppo matura,
Quel che sarò, caduto nella terra?

È nei vivi la strada dei defunti,

Siamo noi la fiumana d'ombre,

Sono esse il grano che ci scoppia in sogno,

Loro è la lontananza che ci resta,

E loro è l'ombra che dà peso ai nomi.

La speranza d'un mucchio d'ombra
E null'altro è la nostra sorte?

E tu non saresti che un sogno, Dio?

Almeno un sogno, temerari,
Vogliamo ti somigli.

Which law is yours?

Blast my poor emotions with a thunderbolt,
Free me from restless thought.

I am tired of shouting without a voice.

2

Languishing flesh
Where pleasure used to throng and thrive,
Heavy-lidded, listlessly waking eyes,
Can you see, my overripe soul,
What I will be, fallen on earth?

The road of the dead passes through the living,

We are the spate of shadows,

They are the grain that splits open in us in dream,

Theirs the distance that is left to us,

And theirs the shadow that gives weight to names.

Is it our fate to be only
The hope of a heap of shadow?

And are you nothing but a dream, God?

We rashly want you to resemble this,
At least: a dream.

È parto della demenza più chiara.

Non trema in nuvole di rami
Come passeri di mattina
Al filo delle palpebre.

In noi sta e langue, piaga misteriosa.

3

La luce che ci punge
È un filo sempre più sottile.

Più non abbagli tu, se non uccidi?

Dammi questa gioia suprema.

4

L'uomo, monotono universo,
Crede allargarsi i beni
E dalle sue mani febbrili
Non escono senza fine che limiti.

Attaccato sul vuoto
Al suo filo di ragno,
Non teme e non seduce
Se non il proprio grido.

Ripara il logorio alzando tombe,
E per pensarti, Eterno,
Non ha che le bestemmie.

It's the birth of lucidest madness.

It doesn't quiver in clouds of branches
Like morning sparrows
At the edge of eyelids.

In us it lives and withers, inscrutable wound.

3

The light that spurs us
Is an ever more tenuous thread.

Do you no longer dazzle, without killing?

Grant me this crowning joy.

4

Man, monotonous universe,
Believes he can expand his goods,
While from his panicking hands
Issue endlessly only limits.

Attached over the void
To his spider thread,
He waits in dread, enticing
Nothing but his own outcry.

He wards off his demise by raising tombs,
And to think of you, Eternal,
He has only blasphemies.

Caino

1928

Corre sopra le sabbie favolose
E il suo piede è leggero.

O pastore di lupi,
Hai i denti della luce breve
Che punge i nostri giorni.

Terrori, slanci,
Rantolo di foreste, quella mano
Che spezza come nulla vecchie querci,
Sei fatto a immagine del cuore.

E quando è l'ora molto buia,
Il corpo allegro
Sei tu fra gli alberi incantati?

E mentre scoppio di brama,
Cambia il tempo, t'aggiri ombroso,
Col mio passo mi fuggi.

Come una fonte nell'ombra, dormire!

Quando la mattina è ancora segreta,
Saresti accolta, anima,
Da un'onda riposata.

Anima, non saprò mai calmarti?

Cain

1928

He runs across the fabulous sands
And his foot is nimble.

O shepherd of wolves,
You have the teeth of the fleeting light
That pricks our days.

Terrors, impulses,
Wheezing rattle of forests, that hand
Which snaps like nothing ancient oaks,
You are created in the image of the heart.

And when the very dark hour comes,
The body buoyant
Is it you among the spellbound trees?

And while I burst with longing,
The weather changes, you wander suspiciously,
At my footstep you flee.

To sleep like a fountainhead in shadow!

When morning is hidden again, my soul,
You'd be welcomed by
A freshly broken wave.

Soul, will I never know how to soothe you?

Mai non vedrò nella notte del sangue?

Figlia indiscreta della noia,
Memoria, memoria incessante,
Le nuvole della tua polvere,
Non c'è vento che se le porti via?

Gli occhi mi tornerebbero innocenti,
Vedrei la primavera eterna

E, finalmente nuova,
O memoria, saresti onesta.

Will I never see in the night of the blood?

Tedium's impudent daughter,
Memory, incessant memory,
Isn't there a wind that carries
Away your dust clouds?

My eyes would be innocent again,
I would catch sight of eternal spring

And, finally new,
O memory, you'd be honest.

La preghiera

1928

Come dolce prima dell'uomo
Doveva andare il mondo.

L'uomo ne cavò beffe di demòni,
La sua lussuria disse cielo,
La sua illusione decretò creatrice,
Suppose immortale il momento.

La vita gli è di peso enorme
Come liggiù quell'ale d'ape morta
Alla formicola che la trascina.

Da ciò che dura a ciò che passa,
Signore, sogno fermo,
Fa' che torni a correre un patto.

Oh! rasserena questi figli.

Fa' che l'uomo torni a sentire
Che, uomo, fino a te salisti
Per l'infinita sofferenza.

Sii la misura, sii il mistero.

Purificante amore,
Fa' ancora che sia scala di riscatto
La carne ingannatrice.

How lovely the world must have been
Before the arrival of man.

Man dug up demons' hoaxes there,
Considered his lust heaven,
His illusion he decreed creative,
He assumed the moment deathless.

Life to him is an enormous weight
As down there the dead bee's wing
To the ant that drags it.

From that which lasts to that which passes,
Lord, unwavering dream,
Renew your covenant.

Oh! soothe these sons and daughters.

Make man feel again
That, man, you climbed to yourself
Through infinite suffering.

Be the measure, be the mystery.

Purifying love,
Make deceiving flesh once more
The ladder of redemption.

Vorrei di nuovo udirti dire
Che in te finalmente annullate
Le anime s'uniranno
E lassù formeranno,
Eterna umanità,
Il tuo sonno felice.

I want to hear you say again
That in you souls will be united,
Nullified at last,
And up above will form
Eternal humanity,
Your blissful sleep.

La morte meditata

1932

CANTO PRIMO

O sorella dell'ombra,
Notturna quanto più la luce ha forza,
M'insegui, morte.

In un giardino puro
Alla luce ti diè l'ingenua brama
E la pace fu persa,
Pensosa morte,
Sulla tua bocca.

Da quel momento
Ti odo nel fluire della mente
Approfondire lontananze,
Emula sofferente dell'eterno.

Madre velenosa degli evi
Nella paura del palpito
E della solitudine,

Bellezza punita e ridente,

Nell'assopirsi della carne
Sognatrice fuggente,

Death Meditated On

1932

FIRST SONG

O sister of shadow,
Ever more nocturnal the more forceful the light,
Death, my pursuer:

In a pristine garden
Naive craving brought you into the world
And peace,
Pensive death,
Was lost on your mouth.

From that moment on
I hear you in the current of my mind
Deepening distances,
Anguished imitator of eternity.

Venomous mother of ages
In the fear of the heartbeat
And solitude,

Chastised, laughing beauty,

In the slumber of flesh
Elusive dreamer,

Atleta senza sonno
Della nostra grandezza,

Quando m'avrai domato, dimmi:

Nella malinconia dei vivi
Volerà a lungo la mia ombra?

CANTO SECONDO

Scava le intime vite
Della nostra infelice maschera
(Clausura d'infinito)
Con blandizia fanatica
La buia veglia dei padri.

Morte, muta parola,
Sabbia deposta come un letto
Dal sangue,
Ti odo cantare come una cicala
Nella rosa abbrunata dei riflessi.

CANTO TERZO

Incide le rughe segrete
Della nostra infelice maschera
La beffa infinita dei padri.

Tu, nella luce fonda,
O confuso silenzio,
Insisti come le cicale irose.

Sleepless athlete
Of our greatness,

Once you have subdued me, tell me:

Will my shadow's flight last long
Among the sadness of the living?

SECOND SONG

With overzealous blandishment
The dark vigil of our fathers
Unearths the intimate lives
Of our unhappy mask
(Enclosure of infinity).

Death, silent word,
Sandy riverbed deposited
By blood,
I hear you singing like a locust
In the darkened rose of reflections.

THIRD SONG

Our fathers' never-ending jest
Etches the hidden wrinkles
Of our unhappy mask.

You, O muddled silence
In the deep light,
Insist like seething locusts.

CANTO QUARTO

Mi presero per mano nuvole.

Brucio sul colle spazio e tempo,
Come un tuo messagero,
Come il sogno, divina morte.

CANTO QUINTO

Hai chiuso gli occhi.

Nasce una notte
Piena di finte buche,
Di suoni morti
Come di sugheri
Di reti calate nell'acqua.

Le tue mani si fanno come un soffio
D'inviolabili lontananze,
Inafferrabili come le idee,

E l'equivoco della luna
E il dondolio, dolcissimi,
Se vuoi posarmele sugli occhi,
Toccano l'anima.

Sei la donna che passa
Come una foglia

E lasci agli alberi un fuoco d'autunno.

FOURTH SONG

Clouds took me by the hand.

I am burning space and time upon the hill,
like your harbinger,
like dream, divine death.

FIFTH SONG

You have closed your eyes.

A night is born,
Full of spurious holes,
Of muted sounds
Like corks of nets
Dropped in the water.

Your hands turn into a breath
Of inviolable distances,
Elusive as ideas,

And the unsteady moon
And its swaying—lovely, mild—
If you want to place them on my eyes,
Touch my soul.

You are the woman who passes
Like a leaf

And sets the trees on fire in fall.

O bella preda,
Voce notturna,
Le tue movenze
Fomentano la febbre.

Solo tu, memoria demente,
La libertà potevi catturare.

Sulla tua carne inafferrabile
E vacillante dentro specchi torbidi,
Quali delitti, sogno,
Non m'insegnasti a consumare?

Con voi, fantasmi, non ho mai ritegno,

E dei vostri rimorsi ho pieno il cuore
Quando fa giorno.

SIXTH SONG

O lovely prey,
Voice in the night,
Your movements make me
Hot and feverish.

Only you, demented memory,
Could capture freedom.

Dream, elusive and wavering
In clouded mirrors, what crimes
Did you not show me how to carry out
Against your flesh?

With you, specters, I can never hold back,

And my heart is full of your remorse
When day breaks.

Canto

1932

Rivedo la tua bocca lenta
(Il mare le va incontro delle notti)
E la cavalla delle reni
In agonia caderti
Nelle mie braccia che cantavano,
E riportarti un sonno
Al colorito e a nuove morti.

E la crudele solitudine
Che in sé ciascuno scopre, se ama,
Ora tomba infinita,
Da te mi divide per sempre.

Cara, lontana come in uno specchio ...

Song

1932

I see your slow mouth again
(The ocean of nights draws toward it)
And the mare of your loins
Hurtling you in agony
Into my arms that were singing,
And sleep bringing you back
To color and to fresh deaths.

And the brutal loneliness
That all who love discover in themselves,
Now an infinite grave,
Divides me from you forever.

Dear one, far away as in a mirror . . .

Auguri per il proprio compleanno

a Berto Ricci   *1935*

Dolce declina il sole.
Dal giorno si distacca
Un cielo troppo chiaro.
Dirama solitudine

Come da gran distanza
Un muoversi di voci.
Offesa se lusinga,
Quest'ora ha l'arte strana.

Non è primo apparire
Dell'autunno già libero?
Con non altro mistero

Corre infatti a dorarsi
Il bel tempo che toglie
Il dono di follia.

Eppure, eppure griderei:
Veloce gioventù dei sensi
Che all'oscuro mi tieni di me stesso
E consenti le immagini all'eterno,

Non mi lasciare, resta, sofferenza!

Greetings for His Own Birthday

for Berto Ricci   *1935*

Gently the sun goes down.
A too bright sky
Withdraws from day.
It diffuses solitude

As from far away
A stirring of voices.
Hurting if it blandishes,
This hour has strange art.

Isn't autumn's first
Appearance already free?
The lovely season that takes

The gift of folly hurries
In fact to gild itself
With no other mystery.

And yet, and yet, I'd shout:
Fleeting youth of the senses
That keeps me in the dark about myself
And allows the images to timelessness:

Suffering, don't leave me, stay!

Senza più peso

a Ottone Rossi   *1934*

Per un Iddio che rida come un bimbo,
Tanti gridi di passeri,
Tante danze nei rami,

Un'anima si fa senza più peso,
I prati hanno una tale tenerezza,
Tale pudore negli occhi rivive,

Le mani come foglie
S'incantano nell'aria ...

Chi teme più, chi giudica?

Weightless

for Ottone Rosai   *1934*

For a God who laughs like a child,
So much raucous sparrow chatter,
So many dances in branches,

A soul becomes weightless,
The grasslands have such a softness,
Such chasteness revives in the eyes,

Hands like leaves
Are spellbound in the air . . .

Who is frightened now, who judges?

Silenzio stellato

1932

E gli alberi e la notte
Non si muovono più
Se non da nidi.

Starry Silence

1932

And the trees and the night
Don't move anymore
Except from nests.

FROM Il deserto e dopo

The Laugh of the Djinn Rull

The sun is already sinking straight down; everything this hour is suspended and unsettled; every motion is under cover, every sound stifled. It is neither an hour of shadow nor an hour of light. It is the hour of utmost monotony. This is the blind hour; this is the hour of the desert night. The worm-eaten rocks don't stand out anymore, whitish skin funguses in sand. Even the delicate ripples of sand are shipwrecked in the tight weft of rays that are beating down equally from all directions. There is no more sky, no earth. Everything is a scorching and uniform yellow-gray color, in which one strains to move, though as if in a cloud. Ah! if it weren't for that lashing that from the soles of your feet loosens your blood into song, hoarse, melancholy, cursed, you would say this is nothingness. It gets into your blood like the experience of this absolute light that wears itself out on dryness. And from the earth's secret, like an echo of so much suffering, you sense a strangled breaking open of your blood. There is no locust at this hour, not one of those locusts for which, like cats, the nomad is gluttonous. (Remember, in Leviticus, the beautiful names of these little beasts "that have big forelegs above their feet, in order to hop with them over the earth"? "You will be able to eat from every species of grass, from every species of *soleam*, from every species of *argol*, and from every species of *agab*.") No locust at this hour, no chameleon, no porcupine, no lizard, no scorpion; there is no quail, no jackal, no scarab, no horned viper; but I stumble over the skeleton of a *mehari* that will make music tonight when the sea wind whips between its ribs; at that hour it will be like a harrow of the moon; Ualad-Ali will dig into the sand with his walking stick to surprise me, and reveal with a bow the *mehari*'s mummified head; then, without touching it, pushing the sand with his foot, he will carefully cover it back up.

When the rays start slanting, the hour is no less black; but it blinds differently. A mask of shadow issues from a broken place in the steep slope. Whoever has witnessed the wariness of one of these approaching shadows will not find strange the adjective that it suggests to me: robber shadow. It seems not to be attached to anything, to depend on anything, it is removed, and a lover of wordplay might even call it: shadow on the loose. And here I am moved to repeat what has been said by many painters who since the early 1800s have worn themselves out in vain trying to reproduce these effects. If I stare at that shadow, it gathers into itself little by little, it is the nucleus of the picture in the middle of large fringes of swarming light; and if I keep on staring at it, it takes on the glassy and metallic transparency of stagnant water. But flashing with an internal dryness, spent like lime or ashes, it's a water without moisture, a pitiless water: it's not a water which, although unhealthy or contaminated, can soothe thirst: it is a sadistic trick of the light. Where the shadow has been swallowed, two men, I see, are resting with their animals, and their cooked faces waver intermittently, outside of which it may be possible to establish how much distance is between them and the observer, and the tawny sand, and the woolen cloaks; now, everything becomes a blondish wavering, with some fleeting stain like that left by tamarind juice; everything—every visible object—is edged with a yellow singe dying into violet. The distances that can be measured now are all the fruit of distortion: it is the hour of distorted distance. The soil has been so racked and tormented that a deluge of air is hovering over it, hesitant. When a man can stand it no longer, he breaks out in cold sweat; and the desert has this overlay of feverish air. Many different layers are overlapping now in the air. The attenuations of air change as they rise; the highest temperature and the most liquid layer are at the bottom. And now it can happen that a high point of the plain where there might be a tree or some hollowed-out space and a fountain, or where there might not be anything but desolation, though always a semblance of shadow—it happens that the image of that point breaks off from its least shiny panel to rise and be mirrored in a hazier panel, muddling still further our sense of distance. The mirage ... And what is the source of our inmost madnesses if not a distorting separation of image from object?

And when the rays are already quite oblique, and even their refraction is less whole—even then I will have to close my eyes. And why this smoke that I sense under my eyelids, in a blood-red ring? My eyes opened again carefully, I will see the sky; but it won't be possible to say it's clear: over the paling blue, there's a red granulation, and the usual singed edge—yellow dying into violet. And now I know that miles surround me: I know this, but in a strange way: a few steps away from me, people are passing through a swarm of glowing mosquito wings; and I will know that people are in front of me by that halo that hides them and with which they advance, and I will measure the space from the varying intensity of the various haloes, and having reached the hole near the sky—spectral—the people will finally appear to me.

They say that wind is the one and only element of motion and life in these places, said to be of stillness and death. No: the element of life and also the tragic element in the desert is light.

Not that the desert wind isn't a horrendous thing. Here there is the *hamsin*, which I've known since childhood. It's the wind they also call *simun*, sirocco, *sheheli*; it's a nasty wind that arrives here in gusts and whirls from the southwest. I've been hearing it the past two days. According to primitive desert beliefs, those red whirling columns of dust that rush intoxicated over us, and that have a peppery smell that makes you dizzy and depressed, that enter your nostrils and mouth and eyes and the pores of your skin, and that instill in your body, in every cranny of your being, a chafing and a weight as if they were filling you with lead and your flesh were covered with rust that could be taken off only with sandpaper—as the ancient Saharan religion believes, the little granules of sand are dancing djinn, and even today the Tuareg wrap their faces with veils, the *litham*, because of those elementals, those malevolent spirits: so the demon can't enter the body through the mouth and nostrils.

I ask Ualad-Ali:

Does the wind harm many?

He laughs. They don't die from wind. They die from thirst.

When a man sets out on trackless roads, wandering halo, having no other security but the proverb "Fix the pole star in your right eye and follow it until the evening star comes," until Venus comes to alter deceptions, clearing the sky again—when a man sets out behind the star, casting forth a voice neither deep nor high, "Uen, uen, sheh-ikh el Arab, uen?" and he goes away for weeks and months, endlessly casting this singsong, his voice fogged over with light: "Where are you, sheh-ikh el Arab, where, oh where?"—if he goes off the road just a little—thirst awaits him and devours him. Then he will know the final blinding glare. As day falls suddenly on night, the rocks, like Memnon, will make a dry, crunching sound. A foot might sink into the sand, and billions of tiny grains, pounding each other, will make a sound like a drum roll. Rull? He is the black angel! Death by thirst! The laugh of the djinn Rull! *Uen, uen, sheh-ikh el Arab, uen?*

If the Arab returns from the desert, ah! mastiffs are barking in his veins. This is why the nomad is incurable: the desert is a wine, and it is a drug, and it sets a rage on fire that can be quenched only in blood and in languorous loves.

Out of the many senses of death that his thousands-of-years existence has impressed in his veins, the Egyptian has received the saddest sense from the Arab: that the desire for pleasure is a radical thirst, suffering that does not ease up except in madness. This sense: that madness is like an increase of soul, that the soul's prize is liberation into the mortal pleasure of the senses.

Tutto ho perduto

1937

Tutto ho perduto dell'infanzia
E non potrò mai più
Smemorarmi in un grido.

L'infanzia ho sotterrato
Nel fondo delle notti
E ora, spada invisibile,
Mi separa da tutto.

Di me rammento che esultavo amandoti,
Ed eccomi perduto
In infinito delle notti.

Disperazione che incessante aumenta
La vita non mi è più,
Arrestata in fondo alla gola,
Che una roccia di gridi.

I've Lost All

1937

I've lost all of childhood;
I won't be able ever to forget
Myself again in an outcry.

I've buried childhood
In the farthest depths of nights
And now, hidden sword,
It cuts me off from everything.

I remember that I rejoiced in loving you,
And here I am now lost
In endlessness of nights.

Desperation that unceasingly increases,
Life is nothing to me anymore,
Stopped up deep in my throat,
But a rock of outcries.

Se tu mio fratello

Se tu mi rivenissi incontro vivo,
Con la mano tesa,
Ancora potrei,
Di nuovo in uno slancio d'oblio, stringere,
Fratello, una mano.

Ma di te, di te più non mi circondano
Che sogni, barlumi,
I fuochi senza fuoco del passato.

La memoria non svolge che le immagini
E a me stesso io stesso
Non sono già più
Che l'annientante nulla del pensiero.

If You My Brother

If you came back alive to meet me,
Your hand held out,
I could still press,
Brother, in sudden forgetfulness,
A hand.

But nothing of you, nothing surrounds me
But dreams of you, glimmers,
Flameless fires of the past.

All memory unreels is images—
And to myself I myself
Am already no more
Than the obliterating nothingness of thought.

from **Giorno per giorno**

1940–1946

2

Ora potrò baciare solo in sogno
Le fiduciose mani . . .
E discorro, lavoro,
Sono appena mutato, temo, fumo . . .
Come si può ch'io regga a tanta notte? . . .

5

Ora dov'è, dov'è l'ingenua voce
Che in corsa risuonando per le stanze
Sollevava dai crucci un uomo stanco? . . .
La terra l'ha disfatta, la protegge
Un passato di favola . . .

6

Ogni altra voce è un'eco che si spegne
Ora che una mi chiama
Dalle vette immortali . . .

2

Only in dreams now can I kiss
His trusting hands . . .
I chat, I work—
Hardly changed—I'm frightened, I smoke . . .
How can I endure such night?

5

Where is it now, where's the naive voice
Which, racing echoing through rooms,
Eased the worries of a weary man? . . .
Earth undid it, a storybook
Past preserves it . . .

6

Every other voice is a dying echo
Now that one is calling me
From the ageless summits . . .

7

Il cielo cerco il tuo felice volto,
Ed i miei occhi in me null'altro vedano
Quando anch'essi vorrà chiudere Iddio . . .

9

Inferocita terra, immane mare
Mi separa dal luogo della tomba
Dove ora si disperde
Il martoriato corpo . . .
Non conta . . . Ascolto sempre più distinta
Quella voce d'anima
Che non seppi difendere quaggiù . . .
M'isola, sempre più festosa e amica
Di minuto in minuto,
Nel suo segreto semplice . . .

10

Sono tornato ai colli, ai pini amati
E del ritmo dell'aria il patrio accento
Che non riudrò con te,
Mi spezza ad ogni soffio . . .

7

I search the sky for your happy face:
And may my eyes see nothing else in me
When God is moved to close them too ...

9

Ferocious earth, enormous ocean
Divide me from the site of the grave
Where now the martyred body
Is laid to waste ...
No matter ... More and more distinct
I hear the voice of that soul
I didn't know how to protect down here ...
It isolates me, ever more festive and friendly,
Moment by moment,
In its simple secret ...

10

I have returned to the hills, to the loved pines,
And the native accent of the air's rhythm
I'll never hear with you again
Shatters me with every gust ...

12

Sotto la scure il disilluso ramo
Cadendo si lamenta appena, meno
Che non la foglia al tocco della brezza . . .
E fu la furia che abbatté la tenera
Forma e la premurosa
Carità d'una voce mi consuma . . .

14

Già m'è nelle ossa scesa
L'autunnale secchezza,
Ma, protratto dalle ombre,
Sopravviene infinito
Un demente fulgore:
La tortura segreta del crepuscolo
Inabissato . . .

15

Rievocherò senza rimorso sempre
Un'incantevole agonia dei sensi?
Ascolta, cieco: "Un'anima è partita
Dal comune castigo ancora illesa . . ."

Mi abbatterà meno di non più udire
I gridi vivi della sua purezza
Che di sentire quasi estinto in me
Il fremito pauroso della colpa?

1 2

Under the ax the disenchanted branch
Barely protests as it falls—less, even,
Than the leaf at the breeze's caress . . .
And the tender form was battered by
Fury and a voice's
Loving care consumes me . . .

1 4

Already autumnal dryness
Has sunk into my bones,
But, lengthening from shadows,
A demented never-ending
Radiance arrives:
Hidden torment of the sunken
Twilight . . .

1 5

Will I always call to mind without remorse
An agonizing loveliness of the senses?
Listen, blind man: "A soul has left us
Still unwounded by the common scourge . . ."

Will it devastate me less not to hear
The frisky shouting of his purity
Than to feel almost spent within myself
The dreadful shuddering of guilt?

Fa dolce e forse qui vicino passi
Dicendo: "Questo sole e tanto spazio
Ti calmino. Nel puro vento udire
Puoi il tempo camminare e la mia voce.
Ho in me raccolto a poco a poco e chiuso
Lo slancio muto della tua speranza.
Sono per te l'aurora e intatto giorno."

Mild weather, and perhaps you pass nearby,
Saying: "May this sun and so much open space
Soothe you. In the pristine wind
You can hear time's passage and my voice.
Little by little, I have gathered myself
And shut the silent impulse of your hope.
For you I am the dawn and the unbroken day."

Il tempo è muto

Il tempo è muto fra canneti immoti ...

Lungi d'approdi errava una canoa ...
Stremato, inerte il rematore ... I cieli
Già decaduti a baratri di fumi ...

Proteso invano all'orlo dei ricordi,
Cadere forse fu mercé ...

                              Non seppe

Ch'è la stessa illusione mondo e mente,
Che nel mistero delle proprie onde
Ogni terrena voce fa naufragio.

Time Is Silent

Time is silent among motionless rushes ...

Far from moorings drifted a canoe ...
Exhausted and sluggish the oarsman ... The heavens
Already fallen into abysses of smoke ...

Stretched out in vain at the edge of memory,
It may be falling was mercy ...

He did not know

It is the same illusion world and mind,
That in the mystery of its own waves
Every earthly voice is shipwrecked.

Amaro accordo

Oppure in un meriggio d'un ottobre
Dagli armoniosi colli
In mezzo a dense discendenti nuvole
I cavalli dei Dioscuri,
Alle cui zampe estatico
S'era fermato un bimbo,
Sopra i flutti spiccavano

(Per un amaro accordo dei ricordi
Verso ombre di banani
E di giganti erranti
Tartarughe entro blocchi
D'enormi acque impassibili:
Sotto altro ordine d'astri
Tra insoliti gabbiani)

Volo sino alla piana dove il bimbo
Frugando nella sabbia,
Dalla luce dei fulmini infiammata
La trasparenza delle care dita
Bagnate dalla pioggia contro vento,
Ghermiva tutti e quattro gli elementi.

Ma la morte è incolore e senza sensi
E, ignara d'ogni legge, come sempre,
Già lo sfiorava
Coi denti impudichi.

Bitter Harmony

Or at noontime on an October day
From the harmonious hills
In the midst of dense descending clouds
The horses of the Dioscuri,
At whose hoofs a little boy
Had stopped ecstatic,
Above the waves were flying

(Through a bitter harmony of memories
Toward shadows of banana trees
And of giant turtles
Wandering in blocks
Of vast impassive waters:
Under another order of stars
Among strange seagulls)

Off to the plain where the boy
Rummaging through the sand,
His dear fingers soaked
By rain against the wind,
Their transparency inflamed by lightning,
Was clutching all four elements.

But death is colorless and without senses
And, ignorant of every law, as always,
Already was grazing him
With shameless teeth.

Tu ti spezzasti

1

I molti, immani, sparsi, grigi sassi
Frementi ancora alle segrete fionde
Di originarie fiamme soffocate
Od ai terrori di fiumane vergini
Ruinanti in implacabili carezze,
—Sopra l'abbaglio della sabbia rigidi
In un vuoto orizzonte, non rammenti?

E la recline, che s'apriva all'unico
Raccogliersi dell'ombra nella valle,
Araucaria, anelando ingigantita,
Volta nell'ardua selce d'erme fibre
Più delle altre dannate refrattaria,
Fresca la bocca di farfalle e d'erbe
Dove dalle radici si tagliava,
—Non la rammenti delirante muta
Sopra tre palmi d'un rotondo ciottolo
In un perfetto bilico
Magicamente apparsa?

Di ramo in ramo fiorrancino lieve,
Ebbri di meraviglia gli avidi occhi
Ne conquistavi la screziata cima,
Temerario, musico bimbo,
Solo per rivedere all'imo lucido

You Were Broken

The many, gigantic, jumbled, glaucous stones
Shuddering still within the hidden slings
Of suffocated elemental flames
Or in the terrible virgin torrents'
Headlong unappeasable caress—
Above the dazzling glare of sand, relentless
Along an empty horizon, remember?

And the leaning araucaria, huge
With yearning, that opened toward the only
Gathering of shadow in the valley,
Its solitary fibers twisted into flint
More resistant than the other damned,
Its mouth made fresh with butterflies and grass
Where it separated from its roots—
Remember that? a raving silent thing
Above a three-span roundish pebble,
Like magic, suddenly turned up
In perfect equilibrium?

From branch to branch a breezy golden kinglet,
Your hungry eyes on fire with wonder
You made the mottled summit all your own
Musical, impulsive child,
Only to see again along the shining bottom

D'un fondo e quieto baratro di mare
Favolose testuggini
Ridestarsi fra le alghe.

Della natura estrema la tensione
E le subacquee pompe,
Funebri moniti.

2

Alzavi le braccia come ali
E ridavi nascita al vento
Correndo nel peso dell'aria immota.

Nessuno mai vide posare
Il tuo lieve piede di danza.

3

Grazia, felice,
Non avresti potuto non spezzarti
In una cecità tanto indurita
Tu semplice soffio e cristallo,

Troppo umano lampo per l'empio,
Selvoso, accanito, ronzante
Ruggito d'un sole ignudo.

Of a deep and peaceful ocean chasm
Fantastic tortoises
Waking again among the seaweed.

The strain and underwater pomp
Of nature at its most remote—
Deathly warnings.

2

You used to hold your arms out like wings
And give back birth to wind
Running into the heavy unmoving air.

No one ever saw your weightless
Dancing foot stand still.

3

Happy grace,
You were not able not to break
Against a blindness so implacable
You simple breath and crystal,

Too human flash of light for the pitiless,
Savage, unrelenting, droning
Roar of a naked sun.

Nelle vene

Nelle vene già quasi vuote tombe
L'ancora galoppante brama,
Nelle mie ossa che si gelano il sasso,
Nell'anima il rimpianto sordo,
L'indomabile nequizia, dissolvi;

Dal rimorso, latrato sterminato,
Nel buio inenarrabile
Terribile clausura,
Riscattami, e le tue ciglia pietose
Dal lungo tuo sonno, sommuovi;

Il roseo improvviso tuo segno,
Genitrice mente, risalga
E riprenda a sorprendermi;
Insperata risùscitati,
Misura incredibile, pace;

Fa, nel librato paesaggio, ch'io possa
Risillabare le parole ingenue.

In Veins

In veins already almost empty tombs
The still galloping longing,
In my bones that are frozen, stone,
In the soul the choked regret,
Untamable iniquity: dissolve them;

From remorse, endless howl,
Terrible seclusion
In the unspeakable dark,
Redeem me, and rouse your merciful
Lashes from your long sleep.

May your sudden pinkish trace,
Mother mind, ascend again,
And return to amaze me;
Come back to life, unhoped for,
Measure inconceivable, peace;

Make it so I, in the balanced landscape,
May mouth again the sounds of artless speech.

Accadrà?

Tesa sempre in angoscia
E al limite di morte:
Terribile ventura;
Ma, anelante di grazia,
In tanta Tua agonia
Ritornavi a scoprire,
Senza darti mai pace,
Che, nel principio e nei sospiri sommi
Da una stessa speranza consolati,
Gli uomini sono uguali,
Figli d'un solo, d'un eterno Soffio.

Tragica Patria, l'insegnasti prodiga
A ogni favella libera,
E ne ebbero purezza dell'origine
Le immagini remote,
Le nuove, immemorabile radice.

Ma nella mente ora avverrà dei popoli
Che non più torni fertile
La parola ispirata,
E che Tu nel Tuo cuore,
Più generosa quanto più patisci,
Non la ritrovi ancora, più incantevole
Quanto più ascosa bruci?

Will It Come to Pass?

Ever stretched in anguish
And at the edge of death:
Terrible fate;
Yet, gasping for grace,
In Your great agony
You realized again, without
Its ever giving You peace,
That in the beginning and in our longing's end,
Consoled by one hope in common,
Men are the same,
Children of only one, one eternal Breath.

Tragic Fatherland, you taught it lavishly
To every free tongue,
And the immemorial images
Had pristine origins,
The new ones, prehistoric roots.

But in the mind of the people will it happen now
That the living word
Won't be fertile anymore,
And that You, more generous the more You suffer,
Won't find it there again
In Your heart, lovelier
The more it burns unseen?

Da venti secoli T'uccide l'uomo
Che incessante vivifichi rinata,
Umile interprete del Dio di tutti.

Patria stanca delle anime,
Succederà, universale fonte,
Che tu non più rifulga?

Sogno, grido, miracolo spezzante,
Seme d'amore nell'umana notte,
Speranza, fiore, canto,
Ora accadrà che cenere prevalga?

For twenty centuries man has been killing You,
Who unceasingly reborn give life,
Humble interpreter of the God of all.

Exhausted Fatherland of souls,
Will it happen, source of All,
That you no longer shine?

Dream and shout, disintegrating miracle,
Seed of love in the human night,
Hope, flower, song,
Will it now come to pass that ashes triumph?

L'angelo del povero

Ora che invade le oscurate menti
Più aspra pietà del sangue e della terra,
Ora che ci misura ad ogni palpito
Il silenzio di tante ingiuste morti,

Ora si svegli l'angelo del povero,
Gentilezza superstite dell'anima ...

Col gesto inestinguibile dei secoli
Discenda a capo del suo vecchio popolo,
In mezzo alle ombre ...

The Poor Man's Angel

Now that the harsher mercy of blood and earth
Fills our darkened minds,
Now that the silence of so many unjust deaths
Judges us at every heartbeat,

Now let the poor man's angel waken,
The soul's enduring gentleness . . .

With the undying gesture of the ages
May he alight before his ancient people,
In the midst of shadows . . .

Non gridate più

Cessate d'uccidere i morti,
Non gridate più, non gridate
Se li volete ancora udire,
Se sperate di non perire.

Hanno l'impercettibile sussurro,
Non fanno più rumore
Del crescere dell'erba,
Lieta dove non passa l'uomo.

Shout No More

Stop killing the dead,
Shout no more, don't shout
If you still want to hear them,
If you're hoping not to perish.

Their murmur is imperceptible,
The sound they make no louder
Than growing grass,
Happy where men don't pass.

Terra

Potrebbe esserci sulla falce
Una lucentezza, e il rumore
Tornare e smarrirsi per gradi
Dalle grotte, e il vento potrebbe
D'altro sale gli occhi arrossare ...

Potresti la chiglia sommersa
Dislocarsi udire nel largo,
O un gabbiano irarsi a beccare,
Sfuggita la preda, lo specchio ...

Del grano di notti e di giorni
Ricolme mostrasti le mani,
Degli avi tirreni delfini
Dipinti vedesti a segreti
Muri immateriali, poi, dietro
Alle navi, vivi volare,
E terra sei ancora di ceneri
D'inventori senza riposo.

Cauto ripotrebbe assopenti farfalle
Stormire agli ulivi da un attimo all'altro
Destare,
Veglie inspirate resterai di estinti,
Insonni interventi di assenti,
La forza di ceneri—ombre
Nel ratto oscillamento degli argenti.

There might be a shining
On the scythe, and the sound
Return from caverns, straying
Gradually, and the wind might
Redden your eyes with other salt . . .

You might hear the sunken keel
Shifting way out at sea,
Or a seagull getting angry pecking,
Its prey having fled, a mirror . . .

You showed your hands filled high
With the grain of days and nights,
And on the secret immaterial walls
Of your Tyrrhenian forebears
Saw dolphins painted, then, behind
The ships, flying alive,
And you're still earth of ashes
Of inventors without rest.

Cautious a rustling in the olive trees
Might again arouse any moment
Drowsing butterflies,
You'll remain inspired vigils of the dead,
Sleepless interventions of those not here,
The force of ashes—shadows
In rapid flickerings of silver.

Il vento continui a scrosciare,
Da palme ad abeti lo strepito
Per sempre desoli, silente
Il grido dei morti è più forte.

Let the wind keep roaring,
From palms to spruces let the din
Forever devastate, the silent
Outcry of the dead is louder.

Canzone

descrive lo stato d'animo del poeta

Nude, le braccia di segreti sazie,
A nuoto hanno del Lete svolto il fondo,
Adagio sciolto le veementi grazie
E le stanchezze onde luce fu il mondo.

Nulla è muto più della strana strada
Dove foglia non nasce o cade o sverna,
Dove nessuna cosa pena o aggrada,
Dove la veglia mai, mai il sonno alterna.

Tutto si sporse poi, entro trasparenze,
Nell'ora credula, quando, la quiete
Stanca, da dissepolte arborescenze
Riestesasi misura delle mete,
Estenuandosi in iridi echi, amore
Dall'aereo greto trasalì sorpreso
Roseo facendo il buio e, in quel colore,
Più d'ogni vita un arco, il sonno, teso.

Preda dell'impalpabile propagine
Di muri, eterni dei minuti eredi,
Sempre ci esclude più, la prima immagine
Ma, a lampi, rompe il gelo e riconquide.

Più sfugga vera, l'ossessiva mira,
E sia bella, più tocca a nudo calma
E, germe, appena schietta idea, d'ira,
Rifreme, avversa al nulla, in breve salma.

Canzone

describes the poet's state of mind

Those bare arms surfeited with secrets have,
In swimming, stirred the depths of Lethe,
And bit by bit set loose the vehement graces
And the weariness that gave the world its light.

There is nothing stiller than that strange road
Where leaves don't bud or fall or winter,
Where nothing ever suffers or pleases,
Where waking never alternates with sleep.

All things leaned forward then, inside transparence,
In the trusting hour, when—the stillness tired,
Re-extended measure of destinations
From the opened graves of branching trees,
Enervating into rainbow echoes—love
Started from the airy riverbed surprised
Turning the darkness rose, and, in that color,
More than every life an arc, sleep, stretched taut.

Prey to phantom tendrils sprung from walls,
Those endless heirs of minutes, the primal image
Excludes us more and more, and yet,
Like lightning, breaks the ice, is lord again.

The more true she flees and is beautiful,
The obsessive aim, the more she touches naked calm,
And, seed—barely pure idea—of fury,
Shudders, opposed to nothingness, in brief cadaver.

Rivi indovina, suscita la palma:
Dita dedale svela, se sospira.

Prepari gli attimi con cruda lama,
Devasti, carceri, con vaga lama,
Desoli gli animi con sorda lama,
Non distrarrò da lei mai l'occhio fisso
Sebbene, orribile da spoglio abisso,
Non si conosca forma che da fama.

E se, tuttora fuoco d'avventura,
Tornati gli attimi da angoscia a brama,
D'Itaca varco le fuggenti mura,
So, ultima metamorfosi all'aurora,
Oramai so che il filo della trama
Umana, pare rompersi in quell'ora.

Nulla più nuovo parve della strada
Dove lo spazio mai non si degrada
Per la luce o per tenebra, o altro tempo.

She presages the streams, makes rise the palm:
Reveals her skillful fingers when she sighs.

Though she ready the moments with blunt blade,
Ravage and hold captive with hazy blade,
Lay waste to spirits with deaf blade,
I will never take my eyes off her, hideous
Though what rises from the barren abyss,
No form is known apart from fame.

And if, still on fire for adventure,
The moments turned again from dread to desire,
I cross the fleeing walls of Ithaca,
I know, by now I know that the thread
Of human story seems to break upon
The final metamorphosis of dawn.

Nothing seemed newer than the road
Where space is never degraded
By light or dark, or other time.

from **Cori descrittivi**
di stati d'animo di Didone

2

La sera si prolunga
Per un sospeso fuoco
E un fremito nell'erbe a poco a poco
Pare infinito a sorte ricongiunga.

Lunare allora inavvertita nacque
Eco, e si fuse al brivido dell'acque.
Non so chi fu più vivo,
Il sussurrio sino all'ebbro rivo
O l'attenta che tenera si tacque.

6

Tutti gl'inganni suoi perso ha il mistero,
A vita lunga solita corona,
E, in se stesso mutato,
Concede il fiele dei rimorsi a gocce.

7

Nella tenebra, muta
Cammini in campi vuoti d'ogni grano:
Altero al lato tuo più niuno aspetti.

from **Choruses Descriptive of Dido's States of Mind**

2

Evening is prolonged by hanging fire
And a shudder in the grass
Little by little seems to reconcile
Fate and infinity.

Then, like moonlight, unobserved, Echo was born
And melded with the waters' trembling.
I don't know which was more alive:
The gurgling up to the drunken stream
Or the attentive one who tenderly was silent.

6

Mystery has lost all its illusions,
A long life's usual crown,
Which transformed now into itself,
Surrenders drops of rancorous regret.

7

Silent in the darkness
You walk in fields barren of all grain:
Waiting for no one at your haughty side.

10

Non odi del platano,
Foglia non odi a un tratto scricchiolare
Che cade lungo il fiume sulle selci?

Il mio declino abbellirò, stasera;
A foglie secche si vedrà congiunto
Un bagliore roseo.

16

Non sfocerebbero ombre da verdure
Come nel tempo ch'eri agguato roseo
E tornava a distendersi la notte
Con i sospiri di sfumare in prato,
E a prime dorature ti sfrangiavi,
Incerte, furtiva, in dormiveglia.

17

Trarresti dal crepuscolo
Un'ala interminabile.
Con le sue piume più fugaci
A distratte strie ombreggiando,
Senza fine la sabbia
Forse ravviveresti.

1 0

Don't you hear from the plane tree,
Don't you suddenly hear a leaf scraping
That falls on the flagstones along the river?

I will beautify my going-down, this evening;
To dry leaves will be joined
A rosy gleam.

1 6

No more inlets of shadow pouring forth from green
As in the days when you were a rosy ambush,
And night returned to lie down
With sighs of spreading darkness in the field.
And at the first uncertain gildings you
Frayed, furtive, half asleep.

1 7

You might drag an interminable wing
Out of twilight.
With its most transient feathers
Shedding shadows in distracted grooves,
Perhaps you might endlessly
Revive the sand.

18

Lasciò i campi alle spighe l'ira avversi,
E la città, poco più tardi,
Anche le sue macerie perse.

Àrdee errare cineree solo vedo
Tra paludi e cespugli,
Terrorizzate urlanti presso i nidi
E gli escrementi dei voraci figli
Anche se appaia solo una cornacchia.

Per fetori s'estende
La fama che ti resta,
Ed altro segno più di te non mostri
Se non le paralitiche
Forme della viltà
Se ai tuoi sgradevoli gridi ti guardo.

19

Deposto hai la superbia negli orrori,
Nei desolati errori.

1 8

Rage left the fields hostile to ears of grain,
And the city, a little later,
Lost even its ruins.

I see only errant ash-gray herons
Among swamps and bushes,
Shrieking panic-stricken close to nests
And the droppings of their voracious young
Even should only a crow appear.

Through stenches extends
The fame that remains to you,
And you display no other trace of yourself
Beyond the paralytic shapes
Of cowardice, if, because
Of your unpleasant shouts, I look at you.

1 9

You left your pride in the horrors,
The desolate errors.

Variazioni su nulla

Quel nonnulla di sabbia che trascorre
Dalla clessidra muto e va posandosi,
E, fugaci, le impronte sul carnato,
Sul carnato che muore, d'una nube . . .

Poi mano che rovescia la clessidra,
Il ritorno per muoversi, di sabbia,
Il farsi argentea tacito di nube
Ai primi brevi lividi dell'alba . . .

La mano in ombra la clessidra volse,
E, di sabbia, il nonnulla che trascorre
Silente, è unica cosa che ormai s'oda
E, essendo udita, in buio non scompaia.

Variations on Nothing

That negligible bit of sand which slides
Without a sound and settles in the hourglass,
And the fleeting impressions on the fleshy-pink,
The perishable fleshy-pink, of a cloud . . .

Then a hand that turns over the hourglass,
The going back for flowing back, of sand,
The quiet silvering of a cloud
In the first few lead-gray seconds of dawn . . .

The hand in shadow turned the hourglass,
And the negligible bit of sand which slides
And is silent, is the only thing now heard,
And, being heard, doesn't vanish in the dark.

Il taccuino del vecchio

Dialogo

Nuove

The Old Man's Notebook

Dialogue

New Things

from **Ultimi cori**
per la Terra Promessa

Roma, 1952–1960

1

Agglutinati, all'oggi
I giorni del passato
E gli altri che verranno.

Per anni e lungo secoli
Ogni attimo sorpresa
Nel sapere che ancora siamo in vita,
Che scorre sempre come sempre il vivere,
Dono e pena inattesi
Nel turbinìo continuo
Dei vani mutamenti.

Tale per nostra sorte
Il viaggio che proseguo,
In un battibaleno
Esumando, inventando
Da capo a fondo il tempo,
Profugo come gli altri
Che furono, che sono, che saranno.

3

Quando un giorno ti lascia,
Pensi all'altro che spunta.

from **Last Choruses**
for the Promised Land

Rome, 1952–1960

1

The days that are past
And the others to come
Gathered, in the present.

For years and through the centuries
A surprise at every moment
In the knowledge we are still in life,
That living ever flows, always flowing,
Unexpected gift and pain
In the continuous whirl
Of empty change.

Such in keeping with our fate
Is this journey I continue,
In the flash of an instant
Unearthing and inventing
Time from first to last,
Refugee like all the others
Who have been, who are, who are to come.

3

When one day leaves you,
Ponder the other one poking into view.

È sempre pieno di promesse il nascere
Sebbene sia straziante
E l'esperienza d'ogni giorno insegni
Che nel legarsi, sciogliersi o durare
Non sono i giorni se non vago fumo.

5

Si percorre il deserto con residui
Di qualche immagine di prima in mente,

Della Terra Promessa
Nient'altro un vivo sa.

7

Se una tua mano schiva la sventura,
Con l'altra mano scopri
Che non è il tutto se non di macerie.

È sopravvivere alla morte, vivere?

Si oppone alla tua sorte una tua mano,
Ma l'altra, vedi, subito t'accerta
Che solo puoi afferrare
Bricioli di ricordi.

Beginning is always full of promise
Though it torments us
And the experience of every day teaches
That in binding, setting free, or lasting
The days are only drifting smoke.

5

We pass through the desert with vestiges
Of some earlier image in our mind,

A living man knows nothing more
About the Promised Land.

7

If one of your hands avoids misfortune,
With the other hand you find
That nothing can be whole that isn't rubble.

Surviving death—is that living?

One of your hands opposes your fate,
But the other, see, confirms at once
That you can only get hold
Of scraps of memory.

8

Sovente mi domando
Come eri ed ero prima.

Vagammo forse vittime del sonno?

Gli atti nostri eseguiti
Furono da sonnambuli, in quei tempi?

Siamo lontani, in quell'alone d'echi,
E mentre in me riemergi, nel brusìo
Mi ascolto che da un sonno ti sollevi
Che ci previde a lungo.

9

Ogni anno, mentre scopro che Febbraio
È sensitivo e, per pudore, torbido,
Con minuto fiorire, gialla irrompe
La mimosa. S'inquadra alla finestra
Di quella mia dimora d'una volta,
Di questa dove passo gli anni vecchi.

Mentre arrivo vicino al gran silenzio,
Segno sarà che niuna cosa muore
Se ne ritorna sempre l'apparenza?

O saprò finalmente che la morte
Regno non ha che sopra l'apparenza?

8

Often I wonder about
How you and I once were.

Were we wandering victims of sleep perhaps?

Were the actions we carried out
In those days like sleepwalking?

We are far away inside that halo of echoes,
And while you emerge again in me, I listen to myself
In the murmur that you are rising from a sleep
That long foresaw us.

9

Every year, when I discover that February
Feels intensely and, for modesty's sake, is muddy,
The mimosa erupts, yellow
With tiny blossoms. It's framed in the window
Of that, my former home,
And this one, where I'm spending my old age.

As I approach the great silence,
Will it be a sign that no thing dies
If its appearance keeps coming back?

Or will I finally know that death
Is sovereign over nothing but appearance?

11

È nebbia, acceca vaga, la tua assenza,
È speranza che logora speranza,

Da te lontano più non odo ai rami
I bisbigli che prodigano foglie
Con ugole novizie
Quando primaverili arsure provochi
Nelle mie fibre squallide.

16

Da quella stella all'altra
Si carcera la notte
In turbinante vuota dismisura,

Da quella solitudine di stella
A quella solitudine di stella.

18

Per sopportare il chiaro, la sua sferza,
Se il chiaro apparirà,

Per sopportare il chiaro, per fissarlo
Senza battere ciglio,
Al patire ti addestro,
Espìo la tua colpa,

1 1

It's fog, it floats and blinds, your absence,
It's hope that wears hope down,

Far from you I no longer hear in branches
The murmurs leaves pour forth
With budding voices
When you arouse spring fever
In my dismal flesh.

1 6

From that star to the other
Night is held captive
In eddying empty excess

From the loneliness of that star
To the loneliness of the other.

1 8

To endure the light, the lash of it,
If light appears,

To endure the light, to gaze on it
Without batting an eye,
I inure you to suffering,
I expiate your guilt,

Per sopportare il chiaro
La sferza gli contrasto
E ne traggo presagio che, terribile,
La nostra diverrà sublime gioia!

1 9

Veglia e sonno finiscano, si assenti
Dalla mia carne stanca,
D'un tuo ristoro, senza tregua spasimo.

2 1

Darsi potrà che torni
Senza malizia, bimbo?

Con occhi che non vedano
Altro se non, nel mentre a luce guizza,
Casta l'irrequietezza della fonte?

2 3

In questo secolo della pazienza
E di fretta angosciosa,
Al cielo volto, che si doppia giù
E più, formando guscio, ci fa minimi
In sua balìa, privi d'ogni limite,
Nel volo dall'altezza
Di dodici chilometri vedere

To endure the light
I set the lash against it,
Gleaning the omen that our terrifying joy
Will one day be sublime!

19

May wakefulness and sleeping end, may
This ceaseless wrenching for want
Of your solace, quit my tired flesh.

21

Could it be that I'll be guileless
Again, a child?

With eyes that don't see
Anything but, rising into light,
The chaste pulsations of springwater?

23

In this century of patience
And anguished haste,
Facing the sky that is doubled below
And more, forming a shell, makes us tiny
In its power, lacking every limit,
Flying at the height
Of twelve kilometers you can

Puoi il tempo che s'imbianca e che diventa
Una dolce mattina,
Puoi, non riferimento
Dall'attorniante spazio
Venendo a rammentarti
Che alla velocità ti catapultano
Di mille miglia all'ora,
L'irrefrenabile curiosità
E il volere fatale
Scordandoti dell'uomo
Che non saprà mai smettere di crescere
E cresce già in misura disumana,
Puoi imparare come avvenga si assenti
Uno, senza mai fretta né pazienza
Sotto veli guardando
Fino all'incendio della terra a sera.

24

Mi afferri nelle grinfie azzurre il nibbio
E, all'apice del sole,
Mi lasci sulla sabbia
Cadere in pasto ai corvi.

Non porterò più sulle spalle il fango,
Mondo mi avranno il fuoco,
I rostri crocidanti
L'azzannare afroroso di sciacalli.

Poi mostrerà il beduino,
Dalla sabbia scoprendolo

See the time that whitens and becomes
A lovely morning,
You can, no reference point
From the encompassing space
Coming to remind you
That you are being catapulted
At a thousand miles an hour,
Forgetting the brakeless curiosity
And fatal will of man
Who will never know how to stop growing
And indeed is growing to inhuman size,
You can find out how it comes about
That a man may take his leave
With neither haste nor patience,
Looking under veils until
The burning of the earth at evening.

2 4

Let the kite snatch me up in its blue talons
And, at the zenith of the sun,
Drop me on the sand
As food for crows.

I will no longer shoulder mud,
I will be purified by fire,
The pointed squawking beaks,
The reeking ripping fangs of jackals.

Then the Bedouin will bring to light,
Laying bare in sand that he pokes

Frugando col bastone,
Un ossame bianchissimo.

2 6

Soffocata da rantoli scompare,
Torna, ritorna, fuori di sé torna,
E sempre l'odo più addentro di me
Farsi sempre più viva,
Chiara, affettuosa, più amata, terribile,
La tua parola spenta.

2 7

L'amore più non è quella tempesta
Che nel notturno abbaglio
Ancora mi avvinceva poco fa
Tra l'insonnia e le smanie,

Balugina da un faro
Verso cui va tranquillo
Il vecchio capitano.

Around in with his walking stick,
A pure white mound of bones.

2 6

Choked by gasping breath it disappears,
Returns, returns again, returns delirious,
And I hear it ever more inside myself,
Becoming more and more alive,
Clear, affectionate, more beloved, fearsome:
Your extinguished word.

2 7

Love is no longer that tempest
Which in nocturnal blindness
Still enthralled me not long ago
Between insomnia and crazy craving,

It flickers from a beacon
Toward which sails, serene,
The aged captain.

Per sempre

Roma, il 24 Maggio 1959

Senza niuna impazienza sognerò,
Mi piegherò al lavoro
Che non può mai finire,
E a poco a poco in cima
Alle braccia rinate
Si riapriranno mani soccorrevoli,
Nella cavità loro
Riapparsi gli occhi, ridaranno luce,
E, d'improvviso intatta
Sarai risorta, mi farà da guida
Di nuovo la tua voce,
Per sempre ti rivedo.

Forever

Rome, May 24, 1959

Without impatience I'll dream,
I'll bend to the task
That can never end,
And little by little at the tips
Of reborn arms
Succoring hands will reopen,
The eyes reappeared
In their sockets will give light again
And, suddenly intact,
You'll have resurrected, your voice
Will be my guide again,
I'm seeing you again forever.

12 settembre 1966

Sei comparsa al portone
In un vestito rosso
Per dirmi che sei fuoco
Che consuma e riaccende.

Una spina mi ha punto
Delle tue rose rosse
Perché succhiassi al dito,
Come già tuo, il mio sangue.

Percorremmo la strada
Che lacera il rigoglio
Della selvaggia altura,
Ma già da molto tempo
Sapevo che soffrendo con temeraria fede,
L'età per vincere non conta.

Era di lunedì,
Per stringerci le mani
E parlare felici
Non si trovò rifugio
Che in un giardino triste
Della città convulsa.

September 12, 1966

You showed up at the door
In a red dress
To tell me you're fire
That consumes and reignites.

A thorn of your red roses
Pricked me, so that you
Might suck my finger
As if my blood were already yours.

We walked the length of the street
That rips the fullness
Of the savage height,
But I knew already long ago
That, suffering with reckless faith,
Age doesn't matter for winning.

It was a Monday,
To hold hands
And talk together happy
The only refuge we found
Was in a sad garden
Of the hectic city.

La conchiglia

1

A conchiglia del buio
Se tu, carissima, accostassi
Orecchio d'indovina,
Per forza ti dovresti domandare:
"Tra disperdersi d'echi,
Da quale dove a noi quel chiasso arriva?"

D'un tremito il tuo cuore ammutirebbe
Se poi quel chiasso,
Dagli echi generato, tu scrutassi
Insieme al tuo spavento nell'udirlo.

Dice la sua risposta a chi l'interroga:
"Insopportabile quel chiasso arriva
Dal racconto d'amore d'un demente;
Ormai è unicamente percettibile
Nell'ora degli spettri."

2

Su conchiglia del buio
Se tu, carissima, premessi orecchio
D'indovina: "Da dove"—mi domanderesti—
"Si fa strada quel chiasso

The Conch

If you, my dear, should hold
Your vatic ear against
A conch of darkness,
Then you would have to ask yourself:
"Among a scattering of echoes,
From which where does that clamor reach us?"

Your heart would shudder into silence
If then you closely probed that din
Produced by the echoes
And your fear of hearing it.

It gives its answer to whoever asks:
"That intolerable clamor comes
From a madman's tale of love;
At this point it can be detected only
At the hour of ghosts."

2

If you, my dear, should press
Your vatic ear to a conch
Of darkness: "From where," you'd ask me,
"Does that clamor make its way,

Che, tra voci incantevoli,
D'un tremito improvviso agghiaccia il cuore?"

Se tu quella paura,
Se tu la scruti bene,
Mia timorosa amata,
Narreresti soffrendo
D'un amore demente
Ormai solo evocabile
Nell'ora degli spettri.

Soffriresti di più
Se al pensiero ti dovesse apparire
Oracolo, quel soffio di conchiglia,
Che annunzia il rammemorarsi di me
Già divenuto spettro
In un non lontano futuro.

Which, amid beguiling voices,
With a sudden shudder freezes the heart?"

If you look,
If you look closely at that fear,
My frightened beloved,
Suffering you might tell
Of a mad love
That now can be evoked
Only at the hour of ghosts.

You'd suffer more
If in your thoughts that breath of conch
Should seem an oracle
That presages remembering me,
Already become a ghost
In a future not far away.

Il lampo della bocca

Migliaia d'uomini prima di me,
Ed anche più di me carichi d'anni,
Mortalmente ferì
Il lampo d'una bocca.

Questo non è motivo
Che attenuerà il soffrire.

Ma se mi guardi con pietà,
E mi parli, si diffonde una musica,
Dimentico che brucia la ferita.

The Flash of the Mouth

Thousands of men before me,
And even more freighted with years than I am,
Were wounded to the quick
By the flash of a mouth.

Knowing this won't be the thing
That lessens my suffering.

But if you look at me with mercy,
And speak to me, a music fills the air,
And I forget that the wound burns.

Superstite infanzia

1

Un abbandono mi afferra alla gola
Dove mi è ancora rimasta l'infanzia.

Segno della sventura da placare.

Quel chiamare paziente
Da un accanito soffrire strozzato
È la sorte dell'esule.

2

Ancora mi rimane qualche infanzia.

Di abbandonarmi ad essa è il modo mio
Quel fuori di me correre
Stretto alla gola.

Sorte sarà dell'esule?

È per la mia sventura da placare
Il correre da cieco,
L'irrompente chiamarti di continuo
Strozzato dal soffrire.

Surviving Childhood

1

An abandonment seizes me by the throat
Where childhood is left in me.

Symptom of adversity to soothe.

That patient calling
Strangled by tenacious suffering
Is the fate of the exile.

2

I still have something left of childhood.

My way of abandoning myself to it
Is that crazed running
Gone tight in the throat.

Will this be the exile's fate?

My running blind
Is for soothing my adversity,
The nonstop bursting call to you
Strangled by suffering.

from **Secret Croatia**

Rome, Harvard, Paris, Rome, from April 12 to July 16, 1969

THE STRAITS OF CATTARO

After I lost my father in 1890, when I was only two, my mother welcomed into our home, like a big sister, an old woman who was my ever-so-tender, skillful fairy.

She'd come to Egypt many years earlier from the Straits of Cattaro, where she resided, but she was by birth more Croatian, if possible, than the people from the Straits themselves.

She taught me to divine the wonder that comes to us from dreams. No one will ever remember as many of their fabulous adventures as she did; nor will anyone know better than she how to tell them so they take hold of a child's mind and heart with an inviolable secret that even today remains an inexhaustible source of grace and miracles, today, when that small boy is still and always a small boy, albeit an eighty-year-old small boy.

I found Dunja again the other day, minus the hundred years of wrinkles that veiled and impaired her shrunken eyes, but with the full recovery of her huge nocturnal eyes—fathomless caskets of light.

Now I constantly see Dunja, beautiful, young, appearing in the oases, and the desert, where I wandered so long, can never again surround me in desolation.

I have no doubt that Dunja first leads into a welter of mirages, but all at once the credulous child grows into a child of faith, through the liberations that the truth of Dunja will always yield.

Dunja, the nomad tells me, *for us means universe.*

Renew the eyes of the universe, Dunja.

Ungaretti on Ungaretti

To my late friend Jean Amrouche, who gathered my extempore observations for Radiodiffusion Télévision Française, my first response was, "But this means touching on a very sore spot." "Between one flower plucked and the other given / the inexpressible nothing." It's an obsession that returns often, as the reader will see, in my song. My first impression of consciousness of the very being that I am appears in the meaning of that next-to-nothing. Thus, I was born in Alexandria, Egypt, that is, in a city that's no longer a part of the oasis formed by the Nile. Alexandria is in the desert, in a desert where life has perhaps been very, very intense ever since the days of its founding, but where life leaves no trace of permanence in time. Alexandria is a city without a monument, or better, almost without a monument that memorializes its ancient past. Endlessly mute. Time always carries it away, at all times. It's a city where the sense of time, of destructive time, is present to the imagination first and above all. And in saying *nothing*, I was thinking especially, in fact, of that intense activity of annihilation that time gives rise to there. Also, I was thinking of the mirage that nothingness and abolished time bring about in flashes in the poet's imagination, an imagination that takes me back to childhood, when those mirages first started to be familiar.

I will try to set down a few facts. I lost my father when I was a baby, at the age of two. Thus, I spent my childhood in a house where the memory of my father kept us in a constant state of mourning. It wasn't a happy childhood. My father had left us a rather prominent bakery. My mother ran it. She was involved from sunup to sundown with business and with household goings-on.

She wasn't neglectful; in fact, she took excellent care of her sons. A woman of great energy. I, meanwhile, inherited my father's character, which was opposite to hers. I have a will, yes, but it's a different kind of will. My mother was willful in the extreme, powerfully willful, and didn't naturally let herself be tender.

There are two or rather three elements in my early childhood that took hold of me in the sense of being poetically inspiring. First of all, the night, the night and its traffic: voices of night watchmen: they'd follow one after the other, come nearer, move farther away: *Uahad! . . .* , they came back, *Uahed! . . .* , every quarter hour, their rounds repeated around my infant's ears. It was my first perception of the infinite, of an infinite round, like that of the ancient Egyptians represented in a serpent's biting of its own tail.

Another element of a different sort had to do with the fact that pigs were raised in our courtyard. At night, when it was necessary to wake the Arab workers, when the shift of one or another was up, a laborer from the countryside around Lucca, who stayed in our house after my father's time, went looking for the pig, because usually these Arabs slept soundly, and the pig having showed up suddenly, they were awakened with a start, running away shouting as if possessed. I was offended by that behavior; I felt—and I was only a child—that it was not a good way to act, to desecrate sacred feelings.

Third element. In our neighborhood there was an official of French origin, a Frenchman and a high official in the Egyptian state. He had a son my age. That boy was physically and perhaps also mentally my opposite. He had lost his mother; but the tenderness that he found in his father, and in uncles and aunts, substituted in certain ways for maternal affection. He was very charming, and very affluent in his dress and bearing. He attracted me the way he attracted all of our friends into the big square where we played. He was a kind of king. There was for me that kind of idolatry, and it is perhaps the strongest affection, the greatest friendship that I've had in my life. Nothing I know is comparable to that attachment.

I want to dwell on one of the three elements: mourning. Every week, every single one of them, my mother used to bring me to the graveyard. We went there on foot—it wasn't a short outing, and that part of town was almost uninhabited: some houses around ours; then that very long avenue; and at a certain point the villa of a rich banker, Baron Menasce, sprang into view, and the street was in fact called Menasce Boulevard. At the end of the boulevard, a turn, and right afterward a round, open area, and then, after lots of walking, the graveyard. That walk was endless. My mother would beg or scold me, a little imp never short on fidgety motions to keep under control. We'd reach the graveyard, where we spent hours in prayer that I had to follow, that I had to accompany. Every week throughout my early childhood.

A sense of death, from the very first, and surrounded by an annihilating landscape: everything crumbles, everything, as I believe I've already said: everything has only the briefest duration, everything is precarious. I was prey, in that landscape, to that presence, to that memory, to that constant call of death.

Another moment in my life that is worth mentioning was when I left home to spend several years at boarding school. Those years may have been significant in my moral development, and even beneficial, but in any case I was extremely unhappy in that boarding school. I've always been someone whom nobody could discipline. I find all strictures intolerable.

One morning out of many spent going over lessons or doing homework, through the window of the big room we could see some punished soldiers in an English barracks—punished usually because they'd been caught going around drunk. They were made to walk along a path, and then—I remember it well, it's the sort of thing I can't forget when I happen to have to witness it—the drunken offenders were lashed black and blue. The effect that had on me, of witnessing corporal punishment inflicted on human beings, was an unbearably violent protest in my spirit. The spectacle of flogging at a barracks was one of the most bitter offenses I can recall having witnessed, in the course of an existence long enough to have had to register countless other atrocities.

It's essential for me to talk more about that boy—whose name was Alcide—who personified for me the image of happiness, the boy whom I picture as a hero sprung from my own existence. I was in a boarding school run by priests. One of the founders urged me one day to keep a diary about my life. I did it. I did it, and it was to that boy, who was far away, that I directed almost all the recurring invocations in my analyses of my feelings. One day the priest asks to see my diary, I entrust the notebook to him, which he annotates. He gives the notebook back to me. Immediately after, he asks me not to read what he's written in it. I destroy the notebook. Why did I do it? First of all, I don't like to violate another person's privacy. It's a respect I inherited; I have always observed it. Also, I like there to be something that stays secret for me. I like the fact that, by having respected the secret, it preserves for me a flavor infinitely more poetic than if I happened to know it in all its reality.

Oh, yes, and as for Alcide, something else comes to mind.

At times we broke off our playing in the big square, and the archangel Alcide led us to his house. One day, in the dining room where we'd stopped, was Louise, the daughter of our friend's German governess. She seemed to be waiting for us and invited us to play *poules*, chicken. The fifteen-year-old northerner, her little amazed face; blond, almost albino hair reaching down to her thighs; very long, Cranachian legs. She had us crouch down under the table, as one does out of necessity when no other way of lightening one's load is available. The maiden also crouched down like us, in our midst, and then, one by one, she unbuttoned our little pants and took between her tapering forefinger and thumb, with incredible grace, our little object, which, as is its nature, sprang right up. Ours were undeveloped little things, we were only six or seven years old. She shook her head: "Pouah! Oust! Filez! Un peu plus vite que ça, s'il vous plait! Quoi? Vous avez le toupet de rouspeter, petits nigauds! Hélas? Vos prouesses, on les a éprouvées, gros vauriens!" [Ugh! Hop to it! Let's go! A little more life than that, please! What? You have the audacity to moan, little fools! Too bad? Your prowess, put to the test, big good-for-nothings!] The event didn't damage our innocence, although from that day on it was stretched out in us like a veil. It was a very light, delicate veil, but after all, from that day on Eve had appeared in my life.

Do I perhaps have a tendency to heroize Alcide, dazzling fable from my childhood? He was far away, because he wasn't in boarding school and I was. Later, he too was put away in boarding school, when his father died, some years later. He was far away, and in reality he was an image out of a mirage when he appeared to me. During Easter vacation I was at home: from the window I saw him passing in a carriage with one of his aunts, I believe, and they were going to a shelter for foundlings to bring an offering. I don't know how to say what I felt.

After the death of his father, as I already said, he was in boarding school, and I wasn't at that time. I believe that that boy's birth date was the first of May. Of course, I remember it well, he was born on the first of May, and for his birthday, lo and behold, a sonnet came to me. I don't remember having done others; I've translated many, Shakespeare's for instance, but I didn't make any others. I had that sonnet—in which I expressed a little of all the accumulated feelings that Alcide brought to life in me—delivered to him. He and I were fifteen years old, we were no longer little kids, and the boy was adventurous that evening, he sneaked out of school and came to see me to thank me for the sonnet I had sent him. It is one of the most moving memories of my life.

Afterward I don't know what happened: one took one road, one started out on another, we never saw each other again.

Poetic experience is an exploration of a personal continent of hell, and the poetic act, in being fulfilled, provokes and frees, at whatever price it may exact, the sense that only in poetry can one search for and find freedom. Continent of hell, I said, because of the absolute loneliness that the act of poetry demands, because of the singularity of feeling one is not like others, but alien, like the damned, or as if under the weight of a special responsibility—that of discovering a secret and revealing it to others. Poetry is discovery of the human condition in its essence, that of being a man of today but also a man of fable, like a man from the times of the expulsion from Eden: in his human act, the true poet knows that the act of unknown ancestors is prefigured, in the succession of centuries impossible to go back through, beyond the origins of his darkness.

At this point I think I'm obliged to speak about the most important influences that steered me into poetry. First of all, Leopardi, as far back as when I was fourteen or fifteen. Only later did I reach a point at which I could feel him in all his grandeur and subtle force, that man who preceded Nietzsche, who felt his epoch and perceived our times as perhaps no historian ever had. Not much later, in 1906, I was already a reader of *Mercure de France*, which was, as is known, the review that revealed the new values, every day at that time, and whose audacity surprised even the shrewdest individuals. My reading of *Mercure de France* had an undeniably important effect on my development. The polemic that went on in its pages pivoted around the name and work of Mallarmé. I threw myself into Mallarmé, I read him with passion and, most likely, was not able to understand him to the letter; but literal understanding doesn't count for much in poetry: I felt it. It seduced me with the music of its language, with its secret, the secret which even today is secret to me. Mallarmé is perhaps no longer to me an entirely hermetic poet, he's a poet. Unless I'm mistaken, Racine said it also: before all else, poetry, if it is poetry, seduces by means of the music of its words, by means of a secret.

Racine was for me an author for old people; but I took note of his dominance in poetic expression—when it succeeds in getting into its grip the lantern for penetrating into the psychic labyrinth of the human person, differentiating it from person to person— right away at that time through my encounter with Mallarmé.

With Mallarmé naturally there was also Baudelaire, and how could there not be, if Racine was involved? Baudelaire was the subject of endless discussions with one of my companions, whom they found dead one day, because he had been unable to feel at home in any country, in a room of the same hotel we lived in, on Rue de Carmes in Paris: Mohammed Sceab. The poem that opens *Il porto sepolto* is dedicated to him. He was a boy with clear ideas, and he was particularly fond of Baudelaire. I'm not saying that Baudelaire is a clear writer; he's a writer who loves to roam around inside his caverns, and it's hard to be clear and introspective at the same time, but he's certainly clearer than Mallarmé, and in a word, he's a writer who can be faced without a lot of preparation. My friend's other author was Nietzsche, who had completely taken hold of him. His authors were Baudelaire and Nietzsche; I stayed faithful to Mallarmé and Leopardi: to Mallarmé whom I felt even if I didn't understand him, to Leopardi whom I understood a little more, although he too has, in sublime passages, the necessary hermetic essence.

With Nietzsche I felt a certain connection between some tendencies in my own nature and that which his great name can evoke. I must acknowledge that there's always an eruptive impulse in me to revolt against I don't know what injunctions. I was aware and afraid of this, while at the same time adhering to it, when I was about eighteen years old.

I should say something now about an encounter I had with one of our writers. He wasn't yet a writer but at that time was a marble merchant. He became a writer, I helped him to become one, he can be considered now, today, perhaps the most authentic storyteller of our twentieth century: Enrico Pea. I stayed in touch with him until his death. With his white beard, which surrounded his face as if styled in the fashion of *ulama* and which he never stopped twirling around his big fingers, he had the face of a patriarch, or better yet, one of the Apostles. He was a decade older than me, and besides the marble deposits, he made furniture and had set up for this purpose a mechanical sawmill. Over the sawmill there was an immense room. Pea called that place, because of the color that he'd smeared over its exterior, the Red Shack. Pea was a socialist, and the Red Shack was intended for get-togethers of the revolutionaries who lived in Alexandria or who found themselves passing through. There were young men my age and also older people, from all over the world—Bulgarians, Italians, French, Greeks. Socialists, anarchists. I'd known the anarchists since my early childhood, right in my own house; some of them came to see my family. I saw them again at the Red Shack, those fugitives from forced residence. Egypt was a hospitable country. My mother was not a revolutionary, my mother was scrupulously religious and respected tradition; but she also respected the ideas of others, she had a great respect for everyone. They sat at our table, they ate, they talked with us. They talked about our native region, which I knew about at that time only through hearsay, the wonderful country of hearsay.

In connection with the socialists of Alexandria, I recall an incident. They'd stopped a certain number of Russian socialists and kept them from being sent back to their own country, where in all likelihood they'd have been killed. The revolutionaries of the Red Shack decided, when the train was leaving Alexandria, to go down to the ship and stretch out on the rails to stop the train from continuing on its way, and thus free the prisoners. They did it. They freed the prisoners. There was a trial. The Capitulations were in effect at that time in Egypt, and we were under Italian law. The trial was held at the Italian consulate. No one wanted to convict them; the trial was a formality to satisfy the Russian authorities, who were distasteful to the Egyptian government. I don't remember if there was a general absolution, perhaps there was.

Until that time I knew nothing about Italy except for what I had read in books or learned at home or at school. I knew Italy above all because I spoke Italian, because all that was dear to me was in my language. It's not something that can be explained, but language to me was a tie that brought me to the cradle of my own people in the distant times past.

When I came to Italy for the first time, the most surprising, moving discovery was the mountains. We went with Jahier and a young French writer, Louis Chadourne, to Abetone. The wavering landscape that was familiar to me, the desert, and then the sea, the sea that as a boy I discovered like a derivation of the desert, the sea that was loneliness and nothingness like the desert, that unstable landscape, changeable from moment to moment—disappeared; and in its place the mountains: mountains that stand firm against time, that resist time, that challenge time. That experience was powerfully wonderful, perhaps the most powerful I can remember.

Every time I feel a profound emotion, I feel it because a natural scene has made me know, together with an objective newness, my own newness. Nature, the landscape, the environment that surrounds me always have a fundamental role in my poetry.

Paris is another mirage. It was at that time for all who intended and became or hoped to become writers, or only to complete their studies. But the big discovery for me in Paris was a new color; or better, the shading off into an infinite nuance of color; of how objects, people, the sky, a tree, and everything can vary by degrees into an endless delicacy of color. The grays of Paris. The values of the grays, the fading and kindling of grays. Never melancholic; it's like a perennial reawakening and falling in love, a loveliest of agonies. Arriving there, I was thrown into a state of bewilderment, won over right away by the intimacies of those unspeakable grays.

Milan, where I lived in expectation of the war, is a misty city. I've said many times that from Alexandria I preserved the feeling of the desert, and of the sea that with the desert formed a boundless plain. Italy was revealed to me through the mountains. Paris left me with a memory of delicacy, of a very intimate hermetic delicacy. In Milan it's the fog, and my poems of that period emphasize fog: it's a way of getting myself to sense the muddle in my mind and to transform the fog into a sense of the infinite, so that I might see more clearly.

There's another thing that had no small effect on me. The idea of the East was temporarily erased; the idea of boundlessness, of nothingness, was replaced by the idea of chaos, of interior tumult and disorder. The bustle of the active crowd; and the aspiration to liberty, again an anarchical liberty but, more fundamentally, liberty. In the end, it fell to me to get past every fracture that might foster the revolt of the poet struggling with the external world and to find harmony in myself and in the words thus discovered.

After I disembarked in Brindisi, having left Egypt, and had arrived in Florence, I came across objects quite different from those I'd been used to. I had never cared about architecture. I wasn't at-

tracted to it. I had arrived, I was still very young for many unfa-
miliar things, and in a word, I didn't notice the great buildings that
surrounded me, rare instances of perfect rhythm, I didn't stop to
observe the churches of flawless proportions.

I didn't even pause to observe the streets. I had noticed the
mountains. I learned to know architecture later, seduced by it in
France. And what in France overwhelmed and taught me more:
Saint-Julien-le-Pauvre, or Chartres Cathedral, in short, certain
stages of pre-Renaissance architecture. Still later I found it very
difficult to fit the Baroque in Rome, where I've been living for
about fifty years, into my sensibility.

I have finished learning the meaning of the peerless power of
Rome's architecture, and I love Rome. Today I know well what
that architecture wants to resume. But when I arrived there, it
seemed unbearable to me: I was used to sharp lines, to lines ele-
vated by an inexorable energy, toward the awesome roofs. I had
been used to other modes of expression, and I was able to redis-
cover them in Dante, not in Rome. Perhaps if I'd decided to live in
Florence, I would have rediscovered them there.

Milan is where I wrote my first poems, published for the first
time in *Lacerba*, solicited by Papini, Soffici, and Palazzeschi, who
ran it. I did those poems as, naturally, I had to do them, that is, at-
tempting to represent what was around me in that environment,
what in my feeling was reflected there in that moment, and to ex-
press variations of feeling in the most laconic way possible. Big
discourses have always troubled me. Those poems of mine were
what my poems would be later, that is, poems that have their basis
in a psychological state strictly dependent on my biography: I
don't know how to dream poetically if it's not based on my direct
experience.

When I published *Porto sepolto*, I sent a copy of it to Apolli-
naire, whom I'd known before the war, and from that moment on
our relationship became brotherly. Having received *Porto sepolto*,

Apollinaire wrote to me, and on one of those postage-free post-cards of wartime, he announced that he'd translated the poem dedicated to the memory of Mohammed Sceab. I've never seen that translation.

An unusual coming-together had happened between Apollinaire and me. We felt in ourselves the same composite character and the difficulty that our spirit had in finding the way to resemble itself, to construct its own unity. That unity we would never find in any other way but by turning to poetry. It was the quest, the discovery of a language that liberated if it succeeded in expressing the agonizing search for self.

My regiment had been sent to France to join the army corps under the command of General Albricci. We stopped first at Camp de Mailly. It was desert, the Champagne Pouilleuse, that "miserly" place, as they used to call it. Entirely gypsum, apart from rare, stiff, shriveled pine trees. It's a sad landscape, and there were no barracks for soldiers. We spent some weeks there. Then we were sent to the Verdun front, at that time not a dangerous front. After a while we were transferred to the front at Champagne, no longer the miserly Champagne but the happy one, the one with vineyards. My regiment was lined up precisely opposite Epernay. I wrote some poems during that period. There were hard battles; for us it was not an extraordinary event. What was extraordinary, in that period, was that every so often the soldiers were able to take advantage of leave to go where they wanted. I spent those periods on leave in Paris. And every time, I'd go to see Apollinaire at his house. Those contacts with Apollinaire remain inside me, a memory of catalysts that were to have many consequences in my life and poetry.

Some days before the Armistice, when it was already foreseen, I'd been sent to Paris to collaborate in a magazine meant for soldiers of our army corps. The magazine was called *Sempre Avanti!*

Apollinaire had asked me to bring some boxes of Tuscan cigars, and just arrived in Paris, I hurried toward the house of my friend. I found Apollinaire dead, his face covered by a black cloth, and his wife crying, and his mother crying.

Through the streets they went shouting, "A mort Guillaume!" Apollinaire, too, by heart-rending injustice of coincidence, was named William, like the defeated kaiser.

In 1919 I married Jeanne Dupoix. I believe that's the year of Modigliani's death. We lived on Rue Campagne Première, where at that time there was a really bad cheap restaurant, managed by an old woman the customers called Mamma Rosalie. We'd meet Modigliani at meals there almost every day. He'd arrive with his very young woman, her slender person swathed in a redingote, long and elegant electric blue velvet. Modigliani would hardly eat a thing, he'd send his plate back to the kitchen three or four times, either because he was too full or because he didn't want to see the little bit of meat in his plate that he might have gulped down. He never stopped sketching the people who were there, whenever it flashed into his head, and he'd leave on the table those little scraps of sketches, which then were sold, I think, by the owner of the restaurant. Soutine also came from time to time, and other artists. In short, we were there with my wife and Modigliani at the same table, and Modigliani, whom I'd known before the war, became my friend. And soon, a little while later, came the news that Modigliani was sick, and then very soon he was dead. He died of the illness that was raging at the time, Spanish influenza. He didn't die from alcoholism; maybe alcohol had weakened the resistance of his organism. The very day of his death, his woman, pregnant, threw herself from the balcony.

Among the other encounters that I had in Paris at that time or after the war, those with Soffici and Palazzeschi and the other Futurists were notable; with Boccioni, with Carrà, with Marinetti;

with Braque and Picasso, already Cubists, or with Delaunay, who was known as an Orphic painter; with Péguy, with Sorel, with Bédier, with Bergson. All of them gave me a thousand unmerited warm welcomes in getting together with me, which always surprised me.

They were encounters with a sort of art and a sort of morality that were decidedly important in my general formation and, naturally, in my poetry.

I met de Chirico after the war, but I was perhaps the first Italian to know his *Piazze* directly, the works discovered with amazement by Apollinaire at the Salon des Indépendants, which sent him into seventh heaven. It is those *Piazze* that I was able to get back from the owner of the big sprawling tenement house at Rue Campagne Première, where I lived with my wife right after the war, and then hand over to Breton, who purchased them. I sent the total amount to de Chirico, at that time quite poor. Balla, who today I consider the major Italian painter of our time, I never had the fortune to meet.

Even before *Littérature* was published, I formed friendships with its future directors, Aragon, Breton, Soupault, Tzara. At the same time I met Desnos, still a beardless youth, and started my deep friendship with Paulhan, Paulhan who would become more than a friend to me, a brother. My wife was, for her part, close friends with Alix Guillain, editor of *Humanité*, wife of Groethuysen, an original Marxist theorist, author of the book *Le Bourgeois*, which in those years was a sensational success. My friendship with Paulhan is at once tender, of deep feeling, and intellectual. I collaborated afterward with him, a little at a time, in the literary reviews he did: *Commerce*, financed by the princess of Bassiano, which had as directors Paul Valéry, Léon-Paul Fargue, and Valery Larbaud. When *Commerce*, published from summer 1924 to the end of 1932, stopped publication, the review *Mesures* was founded, with the same intention of supplying clear ideas about all that was happening and new in literature with poetic aims, without distinction of literary genres, in various countries. *Mesures* was published from January 1935 to April 1940. The two reviews published texts of Joyce, Kafka, Musil, and others. *Mesures* had been promoted by an American writer, Church; the editorial board was formed by Church, Michaux, Paulhan, Groethuysen, and myself.

I settled in Italy toward the end of 1919 or at the beginning of 1920. Life was hard, I gave lectures abroad. I gave them in Spain, Holland, Belgium, and at the same time I published travel articles in newspapers, where I spoke about literature and, at times, painting. We lived near Rome, in a little house in Marino, and the worn-out roof in my studio fell down on my head and rain poured in. Our life was hard.

That uncomfortable time was, for my poetry, one of my happy times, the time in which *Sentimento del tempo* took shape, from 1919 to 1935. But the first publication of *Sentimento* came in 1932; the other poems were added later.

From 1919 to the Second World War, by collaborating with *Commerce*, first, then with *Mesures*, by taking part in those literary circles that were the best informed of the time, my experience as a poet kept improving, and my poetry arrived at those expressive qualities that I've developed ever since.

A period thus came to an end that was not made easier by the needs of practical life but that was rich, I think, in results.

Chronology

Notes

Acknowledgments

Index of Titles and First Lines

Chronology

This chronology is mostly a translation of the one that is in Ungaretti's collected poems, published by Arnoldo Mondadori Editore, Vita d'un uomo: Tutte le poesie (Life of a Man: Complete Poems; 1969). I have added some details that I found in Allen Mandelbaum's translation of Ungaretti, Selected Poems of Giuseppe Ungaretti (1975).

1888 Born on February 8, in Alexandria, Egypt, to Antonio Ungaretti and Maria Lunardini, both from the countryside around Lucca. Ungaretti's only sibling, his brother Costantino, was born in 1880. The Ungarettis lived in an outlying quarter of Alexandria, Moharrem Bey, and had a bakery there, which the poet's mother continued to run after the death of her husband, in 1890, from an illness contracted during excavations at the Suez Canal.

1904–06 Until 1905 attends the Ecole Suisse Jacot in Alexandria. During his school years, starts up a friendship with Mohammed Sceab and begins writing poems. Makes first literary discoveries: Leopardi and Baudelaire, Mallarmé and Nietzsche. Follows leading French and Italian literary reviews; often goes to the cafés in Alexandria that are the meeting places for writers and artists; starts a correspondence with Giuseppe Prezzolini, associate of Giovanni Papini and editor of *La Voce* in Florence. Earns some money handling the French correspondence for an importer of European merchandise. In 1906 meets Enrico Pea, also an immigrant to Alexandria, and goes to the Red Shack, a two-story wooden house, painted red, where Pea lived and that he used as a storage place for his marble and lumber business, and which served as a meeting place for political subversives and exiles. See page 248 of this book for Ungaretti's own account of the Red Shack.

1912 Leaves Egypt in the fall. En route to Paris, sees Italy for the first time. In the French capital, where he had intended to study law, attends the courses of Bergson and others at the Sorbonne. At the same time, makes contact with Apollinaire and with other major exponents of the artistic avant-garde: Picasso, Braque, Fernand Léger, Giorgio de Chirico, Blaise Cendrars, Max Jacob, Amedeo Modigliani, André Salmon, and others. In the summer of 1913 Mohammed Sceab, who lives with him in the same hotel on the Rue des Carmes, commits suicide.

1914 On the occasion of the Futurist exhibit in Paris, at the Galerie Bernheim-Jeune, meets Papini, Ardengo Soffici, and Aldo Palazzeschi, who invite him to collaborate on *Lacerba*. At the outbreak of war, moves to Milan, where he forms a friendship with the painter Carlo Carrà.

1915 Publishes his first two poems in *Lacerba*. After Italy's entry into the war, he is drafted into the army and is sent to the Carso on the Austrian front, an ordinary soldier of the Nineteenth Infantry Regiment. Begins writing the poems that will form his first collection.

1916 In December his first volume of poetry, *Il porto sepolto*, is published in Udine, in an edition of eighty copies, solicited and edited by a young officer named Ettore Serra.

1918 In the spring Ungaretti's regiment is transferred to France, on the front in Champagne. At the end of the war, moves to Paris, living on the Rue Campagne Première.

1919–20 Publishes a small volume of verse in French, *La guerre*. Becomes the Paris correspondent for *Il Popolo d'Italia*, which was founded and edited by Mussolini. Toward the end of 1919, *Allegria di naufragi* is issued in Florence by Vallecchi. The same year, marries Jeanne Dupoix. In 1920, leaves *Il Popolo d'Italia* and works at the press office of the Italian embassy in Paris.

1921 Moves to Rome. Makes a living as an editor of extracts from foreign newspapers for the weekly bulletin published by the press division of the Foreign Ministry.

1923 New edition of *Il porto sepolto* published in La Spezia. Moves to Marino, one of the *castelli romani*.

1925 Birth of daughter, Anna Maria (Ninon).

1926 Lectures in France and Belgium.

1930 Birth of Antonio (Antonietto). Death of Ungaretti's mother.

1931 Starts writing travel articles for the newspaper *Gazzetta del Popolo*, in Turin. Writes pieces about Egypt, which he revisits for the first time in almost twenty years, and about Corsica, Holland, and various parts of Italy.

1932 Wins the Premio del Gondoliere in Venice, the first official recognition of his poetry.

1933 Lectures on contemporary Italian literature in Spain, France, Belgium, Holland, Czechoslovakia, Switzerland. *Sentimento del tempo* is published by Vallecchi in Florence and by Novissima in Rome.

1936 A volume of Ungaretti's translations is published by Novissima. The volume contains translations of St.-John Perse, Blake, Góngora, Sergey Yesenin, and Paulhan. Definitive edition of *Sentimento del tempo* is published, also by Novissima. Moves with his family to São Paulo, Brazil, to teach Italian literature and language at the university there.

1937 Death of brother, Costantino.

1939 Death of son, Antonietto, due to complications associated with appendicitis.

1942 Is hired as professor of contemporary Italian literature at the University of Rome; moves back to Italy. Mondadori in Milan begins publication of all of his works, under the general title *Vita d'un uomo* (Life of a Man).

1944 Publishes translations of twenty-two of Shakespeare's sonnets.

1945 Mondadori publishes Ungaretti's *Poesie disperse* (Uncollected Poems), with a critical study by Giuseppe De Robertis and critical apparatus of the variants of *L'allegria* and *Sentimento del tempo*.

1946 Mondadori publishes an edition of forty of Ungaretti's translations of the sonnets of Shakespeare.

1947 Publication of *Il dolore*.

1948 Publication of a volume of translations, *Da Góngora e da Mallarmé*.

1949 *Il povero nella città* (The Poor Man in the City), Ungaretti's first prose collection, is published. At a formal ceremony on the Campidoglio in Rome, is awarded the Premio Roma, a major poetry prize.

1950 Publication of *La terra promessa*, with a critical essay and variants edited by Leone Piccioni. Ungaretti's translation of Racine's *Phèdre* is also published.

1952 *Un grido e paesaggi* (An Outcry and Landscapes) is published in an illustrated edition by Giorgio Morandi.

1956 Shares with Juan-Ramón Jiménez and W. H. Auden the Knokke-le-Zoute International Poetry Prize.

1958 On the occasion of Ungaretti's seventieth birthday, the review *Letteratura* dedicates an issue of 370 pages to his work. Ungaretti's wife, Jeanne, dies in Rome.

1960 Publication of *Il taccuino del vecchio* (The Old Man's Notebook), comprised of poems written after 1952 and a series of testimonies of friends and writers from all over the world. Travels to Japan with his friends Jean Fautrier and Jean Paulhan. Is awarded the Premio Montefeltro at the University of Urbino.

1961 Publication of *Il deserto e dopo* (The Desert and After), a collection of the travel writings done years earlier for Turin's *Gazzetta del Popolo*, plus translations of Brazilian poets.

1962 Is unanimously elected president of the European Writers' Community. Birth of granddaughter Annina.

1964 Lectures at Columbia University in New York.

1965 Publication of his translations from Blake, *Visioni di William Blake*.

1966 Receives the Etna-Taormina International Poetry Prize.

1968 On the occasion of his eightieth birthday, receives a formal tribute by the Italian government on the Campidoglio in Rome. The review *Galleria* dedicates an issue to him. Travels to Brazil and Peru to receive honorary degrees. Publication of *Dialogo* (Dialogue), a volume of love poems illustrated by Alberto Burri, in a limited edition by Editore Fògola in Turin.

1969 The review *L'Herne*, in Paris, dedicates an issue to Ungaretti. Lectures in Sweden, Germany, and various cities in the United States. Is guest of honor at Harvard University, where he lectures and reads. Also lectures and reads at Columbia, the 92nd Street Y, Queens College, the University of Massachusetts at Amherst, and other institutions. Receives honorary degrees from several Italian and other European universities, and awards from the French and Italian governments. A one-volume edition of his collected poems, edited by Leone Piccioni, is published by Mondadori.

1970 A special issue of *Agenda* (London) is dedicated to Ungaretti, with translations by various English and American writers. Travels to the United States in late winter to receive the Books Abroad award at the University of Oklahoma. Falls ill with bronchitis in New York but recovers enough to return to Italy. Is never fully cured of the bronchitis and dies in Milan on the night between the first and the second of June. Ungaretti's funeral is held in Rome at San Lorenzo. Is buried next to his wife in the Campo Verano cemetery. The critic Carlo Bo read the following memorial at Ungaretti's funeral: "The young of my generation, during the dark years of total political and social disillusionment, would have been ready to give their lives for Ungaretti, that is, for poetry."

The translator's text in these notes is in square brackets. The rest is Ungaretti's, which I translated from the notes section of his collected poems, Vita d'un uomo.

L'ALLEGRIA / JOY

[*L'allegria* (Milan, 1931; Rome, 1936) is a collection that incorporates and expands Ungaretti's earlier collections: *Il porto sepolto* (The Buried Harbor; Udine, 1916); *Allegria di naufragi* (Joy of Shipwrecks; Florence, 1919); and a second *Il porto sepolto* (La Spezia, 1923). Each of these volumes expanded the one before, and Ungaretti often revised the older poems as he went along. The following is his prefatory note to all editions of *L'allegria* from 1931 on:]

The poems collected here were written between 1914 and 1919. The oldest of them were published for the first time in *Lacerba*.

For the present, definitive edition, the author has revised the form of his older poems a little, while trying not to alter the directions of his first experiments, even though it may be a rather hopeless undertaking to find a happy medium between the two distant points of human complexity and artistic maturity, while managing to get the different hand to stay hidden. This old book is a diary. The author has no other ambition, and believes that even the great poets had no other ambition, than to leave behind a fine biography. His poems therefore represent his torments with form, but he would like it recognized once and for all that form torments him only because he demands that it adhere to the variations of his spirit, and if some progress has been made as an artist, he hopes it also indicates some perfection reached as a man. He came to maturity as a man in the midst of extraordinary events, to which he was never a stranger. Without ever denying the universal necessities of poetry, he has always thought that, for the universal to be imagined, it must harmonize with the unique voice of the poet by means of an active feeling for history.

[And in the 1969 edition of *Vita d'un uomo*, Ungaretti added:] Since the wolf loses his fur but not his vices, the author who had called the [earlier] editions definitive didn't know how to resist some formal revision with every new chance.

[Ungaretti includes in his notes the following gripping story of how his first book, *Il porto sepolto*, came about. The poems in the present volume that were in the original *Porto sepolto* span from "In memoria" (In Memory Of) to "Commiato" (Envoi), inclusive; see page xv regarding the image of "the buried harbor":]

I began *Il porto sepolto* on the first day of my life in the trenches—Christmas Day 1915. I was in the Carso, on Mount San Michele. I spent those nights lying in mud, opposite the enemy who was positioned higher than us and who was a hundred times better armed. In the trenches, almost always in those same trenches, because we stayed on San Michele even during breaks—the battles went on for a year. *Il porto sepolto* contains the experience of that year.

I was in the presence of death, in the presence of nature, of a nature that I learned to know in a new, terrible way. From the moment that I became a man who makes war, it wasn't the idea of killing or being killed that tormented me: I was a man who wanted nothing for himself but relationship with the absolute, the absolute that was represented by death, not by danger, that was represented by the tragedy that brought man to meet himself in massacre. In my poetry there is no trace of hatred for the enemy, nor for anyone: there is the grip of consciousness of the human condition, of the fraternity of mankind in suffering, of the extreme precariousness of its condition. There is the will to expression, the necessity of expression; there is elation, in *Porto sepolto*, that almost savage elation of vital impulse, of the appetite for living, that is multiplied in the proximity and daily company of death. We live in contradiction.

When I was at Viareggio, before going to Milan, before the war broke out, I was, as afterward in Milan, an interventionist. I can be a rebel, but I don't love war. I am in fact a man of peace. I didn't love it even then, but it seemed that war was necessary to finally eliminate war. They were bubbles, but men sometimes delude themselves and line up behind bubbles.

Il porto sepolto was printed in Udine in 1916, in an edition of eighty copies edited by Ettore Serra. It was entirely his fault. To tell the truth, those pieces of paper—postage-exempt postcards, margins of old newspapers, white spaces in cherished letters I had received—on which for two years, day after day, I had been examining my conscience, sticking them afterward helter-skelter into my knapsack, carrying them to live with me in the mud of the trenches, or making myself a pillow out of them during rare breaks, were not destined for any public. I had no idea of a public, and I hadn't wanted the war and didn't participate in the war to draw applause; I had, and I still have today, such respect for a great sacrifice such as war is for a people, that every act of vanity in that sort of circumstance would have seemed to me a desecration—even that of one who, like us, found himself in the midst of the fray. Also, I had set for myself an ideal so rigorous, and perhaps absurd, of anonymity in a war destined to end, according to my hopes, with a victory of the people, that anything that might in the slightest sense have distinguished me from another foot soldier would have struck me as a hateful privilege and an offense to the people to whom I had meant to give a sign of complete dedication, accepting the war in that most humble state.

This was the state of mind of the soldier who left that morning along the streets of Versa, carrying along his thoughts, when he was accosted by a lieutenant. I didn't have the courage not to confide in that young officer who asked me my name, and I told him that I had no other relief but to search for and find myself in some words, and that this was my way of making progress as a human being. Ettore Serra carried off my knapsack, put into order the scraps of paper, and brought to me one day, when we had finally taken San Michele, the proofs of my *Porto sepolto*.

[The following are Ungaretti's explanatory notes and comments to some of the poems in *L'allegria*.]

Levante/Levant **PAGE 7**
[The poem depicts Ungaretti's memory of leaving Alexandria, en route to France.]
l. 9: *Syrian emigrants*. They were on the ship that brought me to Italy for the first time.
l. 10: *A young man is alone at the bow*. This, of course, is me.
l. 11: *On Saturday evening*. Sudden evocation of Jewish funeral rites that I witnessed in Alexandria.

A riposo/Resting **PAGE 21**
My regiment went to Versa sometimes for days or moments of rest; it depended on the battles.

C'era una volta/Once upon a Time **PAGE 33**
l. 8: *in a far-off café*. This alludes to one of those cafés my friends who did the neo-Hellenic review *Grammata* used to go to, and where Sceab and I used to go to sip our evening yogurt. [The café was in Alexandria. Sceab was Ungaretti's good friend who committed suicide in Paris; see "In memoria."]

I fiumi/The Rivers **PAGE 35**
[The date of this poem is very significant: one day before the end of an important battle, Italy's first victory against Austria at the Isonzo River. The *Encyclopaedia Britannica* says this about the Battles of the Isonzo:

Twelve battles along the Isonzo River on the eastern sector of the Italian Front in World War I. Although it is now located in Slovenia, the Isonzo River at the time ran roughly north-south just inside Austria along its border with Italy at the head of the Adriatic Sea. The river is flanked by rugged peaks, and the Austrians had fortified the mountains prior to Italy's entry into the war on May 23, 1915, giving them quite an advantage over the Italians. The Italian general Luigi Cadorna launched his first attack against the Austrians on June 23. For 14 days the Italian army attempted to cross the river and scale the heights beyond, but they were beaten back . . . In the sixth battle, August 6–17, 1916, Gorizia was captured and a bridgehead was secured across the Isonzo, the first real victories.

Eventually the Germans sent reinforcements to help the Austrian army, and on November 7 the Italian army suffered "one of the worst defeats in Italian history." Ungaretti wrote in his notes:]

Allegria di naufragi is the coming to self-awareness, it is the discovery that first happened slowly, then culminated suddenly in a song written on August 16, 1916, in the midst of battle, in the trenches, and that is entitled "I fiumi." I list there the four sources that mixed their waters in me, the four rivers whose movement dictated the songs that I wrote.

l. 24: *and like a Bedouin.* The Islamic prayer is accompanied by many bows, as if the person praying were greeting a guest.

ll. 36–37: *But those hidden / hands.* They are the eternal hands that shape the destiny of every living being.

[l. 47: *the Serchio.* A river near Lucca.]

l. 60: *and came to know myself.* It is Paris that began to give me, before the more complete knowledge that the war gave me, clearer knowledge of myself, and that had been powerless to grant to Mohammed Sceab, who had come there with me and who was not blessed with starting to know himself without dying from it.

Pellegrinaggio/Pilgrimage PAGE 41

l. 10: *white thorn.* The white thorn, or hawthorn, thrives in every garden of Alexandria. [*Spinalba* is an archaism for *biancospino.*]

Commiato/Envoi PAGE 53

I have always distinguished between *vocabolo* and *parola* [both mean "word" in Italian] and believe that the distinction is Leopardi's. To find a *parola* means to penetrate into the unfathomable darkness of self without disturbing it or succeeding in knowing its secret.

[l. 2: *Ettore Serra.* Ettore Serra was the lieutenant, mentioned in Ungaretti's story about the origins of *Il porto sepolto* (see pages 264–265), who solicited his first collection. "Ettore" is "Hector" in Italian, which also accents the first syllable. The final *e* is pronounced "eh."]

Giugno/June PAGE 59

The landscape of war and that of Alexandria "contaminate" each other in turns.

ll. 13–14: *When will I wake again / in your body.* The allusion is to a woman I loved in Alexandria.

Girovago/Wanderer PAGE 67

This poem, composed in France where I had been transferred with my regiment, dwells on the emotion I feel when I am conscious of not belonging to a particular place or time. It also indicates another one of my themes, that of innocence, traces of which man searches for in vain in himself or in others on earth.

Lucca PAGE 69

[Written in 1919. Ungaretti says that the poem's theme points toward the poems of *Sentimento del tempo.*]

Regarding this poem, the *humor* that sometimes it's said I perhaps put into it, I wasn't expressing a renunciation of the freedom of living, an adaptation to the bourgeois concept of life. In "Lucca" I was pointing out that man is mysteriously called to survive himself in the spiritual order through the word, in the natural order through offspring . . . To accept tradition was and still is for me the most dramatic adventure, that adventure from which develops—right up to the present, in the midst of countless difficulties of expression—my poetry.

SENTIMENTO DEL TEMPO/A SENSE OF TIME

The first edition of *Sentimento del tempo* [1933] was greeted (as in its time, the printing of the first part of *Allegria, Il porto sepolto*) by extraordinary discussions. In two cases I was even honored by the prompt founding of periodicals almost exclusively designed to attack me.

From the hundreds of essays, attacks, commendations, condemnations, I took some statistics. Statistics is the science of our times, and it can be an aid, even in our field, toward some useful consideration of current practices.

Fifty percent of the criticism, for better or worse, was made of observations and judgments mixed together so haphazardly that they demonstrated nothing about their authors but their total lack of logic or complete ignorance of the book . . . under discussion.

In others, everything aimed at reducing to mere hair-splitting the eternal problems of art: content and form, feeling and intellect, and so on. It was no small mortification for me to see my book, too, used as a pretext for such time-wasters.

But ten percent of the criticism helped me to correct many defects, to see more clearly into myself, to better sense my possibilities for development and my limitations.

I would like to draw the reader's attention to one last point. Like *L'allegria*, *Sentimento* is divided into sections. Not by any caprice. Each part of these two books, in its organic complexity, forms a song—with its dialogues, dramas, and choruses—unique and indivisible. Thus, the poems of the "Inni" section—which express a religious crisis, truly suffered, by millions of people and by me, in one of the darkest years after the war—mustn't be separated from one another if they're not to be misunderstood; likewise, the "Leggende" section, and so on; and likewise in *L'allegria*: "Il porto sepolto," "Girovago" [names of individual poems as well as of sections], or any other part of the book.

On the strictly technical side, my original effort was to rediscover the naturalness and profundity and rhythm in the sense of every single word; I have now tried to achieve a harmony between our metrical tradition and the expressive needs of today.

[The "Inni" (Hymns) section that Ungaretti mentions is represented in the current selection by "La pietà" (Mercy), "Caino" (Cain), and "La preghiera" (The Prayer). "Leggende" (Legends) includes "Il capitano" (The Captain) through "Dove la luce" (Where the Light). It was impossible to maintain the structure he describes; I have, however, preserved the order of the poems in *Vita d'un uomo*.

[Ungaretti wrote an introductory essay to *Sentimento del tempo*, included in the notes section of *Vita d'un uomo*, which I translate here for readers interested in his ideas about Rome and the Baroque. See pages xxvi–xxvii for a little more about this important aspect of Ungaretti's imagination and thinking.]

Tradition—since we are bound to have to discuss it—was a gradual conquest of its values during the years in which I began the extremely slow distillation, if you will, of my *Sentimento del tempo*.

When I arrived in Rome to settle down there, I had already been all over Europe, and at that time Rome was different. It would end up becoming my city, but when I was newly arrived, it seemed to me a place I might never get used to. Its monuments, its history, all that it possessed of greatness, perhaps, surely of greatness—there was absolutely nothing familiar about it to me. It became my city when I arrived at an understanding of what the Baroque is, what has baroqueness, what there is, at bottom, to the Baroque. Because Rome is basically that, it is basically a Baroque city. And the difficulty I had trouble overcoming at first was in seeing that there was a unity in the city. A great one, Michelangelo, showed me the way, because the Roman Baroque was brought into being by Michelangelo. The Baths of Diocletian, the Church of Santa Maria degli Angeli, the Campidoglio with the Tarpeian Rock, and also the *Last Judgment* in the Sistine Chapel are works where Michelangelo mixes everything, mixes nature, mixes Plato with the Renaissance disciples of Plotinus, has a desperate awareness of Christ and, at the same time, an equally desperate awareness of flesh. Such elements, which present a lingering wound, a lingering split in their union, are the elements that Michelangelo brought together in his work and that we discover everywhere in Rome, from the day his earthly passage there came to an end.

The man of pain and the man obscurely in meditation on justice and mercy: absolute contradiction, dialectic of opposites. The awesome Justice of the *Last Judgment* in the Sistine Chapel is placed in opposition to the *Pietà*, which depicts the very moment of the act that professes the Passion and Crucifixion of the Son of God made man, or, if you wish, of the Son of Man raised to God by unmerited but accepted suffering. Christ, God and man, being judge and victim, it follows that justice and mercy are two ways to read the same divine text, in the unfathomable mystery through which God is revealed and hidden at the same time.

Michelangelo revealed to me, therefore, the secret of the Baroque. It is not an abstract notion that can be defined in a logical proposition. It is a secret of the inner life, and my long intimacy with that Baroque, which a little while earlier was so foreign to me, made me capable of accepting all the discrepancies, all the internal tensions, all those givens that man can finally fuse within his own genius, if I had any.

Until 1932, my poetry took shape above all by observing the landscape, observing Rome through all the changes of the seasons, Rome or the countryside near Rome. Whoever follows the poems of *Sentimento* will see that almost all the ones in the first part [through "Ricordo d'Affrica" in the present volume] describe summer landscapes, summer being at that time my favorite season. I loved and still love summer, but it is distant from my bones, it is no longer my season. They are summer landscapes, violent beyond measure, where the air is pure, and they have the character to which I had adapted myself, the character of the Baroque, since summer is the baroque season. The Baroque is something that has leaped into the air, that has crumbled into a thousand pieces: it is a new thing that is remade with those crumbs and that regains wholeness, reality. Summer is like the Baroque: it crumbles and comes together again.

Autumns come a little later, with *La terra promessa*. If there is some springtime memory in those poems, for example, in "Senza più peso" [Weightless]—it's the exception: there was nothing in those years but summer. In those years I couldn't grasp nature except when it was prey to the sun and burned the travertine, rock with which Rome was built, that follows the seasons, that embodies them and in summer is stone that is all dried up. Then in autumn it catches fire, and in winter it is dismal. Stone very subject to change by the effects of the light: when night is moonless, it has the quality of etchings. Stone lives, and the character of that stone was more familiar to me than the ruins, than lines of architecture; it was more familiar to me than history with its monuments.

When I set to work on *Sentimento*, two poets were my favorites: still Leopardi and Petrarch. What did those two poets represent for me? Leopardi in his poetry had manifested with desperation the sense of decadence; he had felt that the duration of the civilization to which he felt connected had reached its final moment and was ready to be transformed from top to bottom. Something was perishing; forms, at the same time, were perishing. A language became conscious of its own aging.

Petrarch had found himself in a different situation: he was facing an ancient literature, the classics, that needed to be added to the circulation of living languages in order to give them roots. It wasn't a matter of discovering historical continuity but simply of basing a new language on established foundations. The movement was different: Petrarch found himself—and here is how Rome happened to become my city—in the presence of ruins, and his memory, the memory of a man who wanted to illuminate once again with a renewed grasp of ancient experience the memory not afforded him by that ancientness so in ruins, so mutilated in appearance.

When Leopardi acquired the sense of decadence, what he had before his eyes was what, in its own renewal, its own impulse, had done nothing but gradually lose energy. Therefore, on the one hand a poetry effect of mutilation, on the other hand a poetry effect of the consciousness that the renovation due to that mutilation had been genuine and had propagated a state that should have been renewed but was constantly losing energy and heading toward death. That was what I learned looking around Rome, where those feelings were present, whether in the ruins or in the memoried structures, signs that many things had perished and were dying more and more.

In *Sentimento del tempo* there is an almost systematic recourse to mythology that couldn't exist in any way in *L'allegria*. There were no more Apollos in the second part of *Sentimento*, or Junos; but living in Rome, in Lazio, how could I not become familiar with the myths, the ancient myths? I met them everywhere, constantly, and they quickly and naturally came to represent my moods. They were voices of the lexicon rushed to evoke the phantasms that frequently appeared to me in the town where I lived. They were not rhetorical figures but a kind of appropriation of myths that became very familiar to me by making me write a poem like "Giunone" [Juno] where who knows what erotic recourse is hidden. It's essential also to consider the Baroque in its metaphysical and religious aspect—that is, in its relationship to man as prey and at the same time to the exaltation of his own fantastic maker's infallibility and to the sense of the precariousness of his condition. The two aspects are constant conditions of life—that is, creation and destruction, life and death. What could poetry be if not the unending quest and never-arrived-at solution of the source of all that? In short, in the contemplation of the Baroque, little by little my poetry tended toward a presentation of the religious problem.

Sentimento del tempo is in fact a book that can be divided into two moments. In the first is the taking possession of a city that I had to make mine, since my native city is a foreign city; and Rome became familiar to my feeling more than any other, shaping it through the passing of the seasons and above all through the forcefulness of its summers. In the second moment of *Sentimento*, Rome again is at the center of my meditations. Rome became in my poetry that city where my religious experience was rediscovered via an unexpected kind of initiation. Certainly, ever since its inception, my poetry has been entirely and genuinely a basically religious poetry. I had always meditated on the problems of man and his relationship with the eternal, on the problems of the ephemeral and of history. I returned later on, because of the extremely grave crisis in which we struggle, to deep meditation on those same problems. It was again the Baroque that helped me.

Rome, in the years during which I was writing *Sentimento*, was a city where the feeling of eternity was still to be had, and not even today, in the mind's eye, has it vanished in front of certain ruins. When one is in the presence of the Colosseum, an enormous cylinder with empty eye sockets, one has the sense of emptiness. Naturally, having the sense of emptiness, one cannot help but also have the dread of emptiness. Those things piled up, coming from every direction, so that not a bit of space is left, of free space, everything is filled, nothing is left, nothing freed. That dread of emptiness, one can feel it in Rome infinitely more than in any other place on earth, more even than in the desert. I believe that from the dread of emptiness issues, not the need of filling that space with it-matters-not-what-thing, but all the drama of the art of Michelangelo.

When I said that the Baroque provoked the sense of emptiness, that the aesthetic of the Roman Baroque had been initiated by the dread of emptiness, I mentioned the Colosseum. I'm afraid I haven't been clear enough. The dread in the Baroque originated with the intolerable idea of a body without a soul. A skeleton evokes the dread of emptiness.

When Michelangelo represents Christ in his last work, the *Rondanini Pietà*, Christ is a soulless body, an empty body, and in that effect of justice, Michelangelo sees nothing but dread. He doesn't picture the *Pietà* in terms of the mother who at all cost wants to revive her child. The Apocalypse had shown to Michelangelo Christ the Judge. It represented him interpreting sacred texts. It was the idea of the terrible Christ that came to him from the idea of death. He didn't arrive at an acknowledgment of death; nor did any of the great artists who came after Michelangelo do so. Resurrection is an idea that is not successfully assimilated. Michelangelo was a good Christian, but . . . was he really a Christian? It's a question no one would know how to respond to . . . Emptiness and space are not at all identical notions. In any form, for example, that man has invented, built, appropriated with poetry or architecture or painting, there is always a kind of abyss that attracts him in the form's interior. There is always in his work, as in himself, an absence, and that absence produces vertigo, fear. And man in a state of vertigo—which would be like the material, spatial definition of the absence of being—responds with his frenzy of activity, in particular acting as poet, as artist. In this regard I think of Petrarch. Petrarch starts with the idea of absence. Laura is an absent world, a world to regain. It is regained by having recourse to poetry, making available again to our language the experience of the ancient tongue, the classical languages. But absence is one thing, emptiness is another. There is a living form that is absent, or else there is no living form, and there is emptiness. It is distinct, a different mode of feeling.

I said a little while back that Michelangelo invented emptiness, since emptiness as poetic inspiration first appears with him. I have to specify the idea of absence. The idea of absence that Petrarch conceived of is quite another matter, it is a world remote in space and time that returns to be heard living in the midst of the foliage of feeling, memory, and fantasy. It is above all a rupture in the darkness of memory.

Is the sensation of the radical absence of being perhaps, in reality, the sensation of divine absence? Can only God eliminate emptiness, He, the Being, He, the Plenitude? Is the feeling of the absence of God in us represented not symbolically but in reality by the dread of emptiness, by that vertigo, by that terror? Michelangelo and some other men in Italy from the end of the Quattrocento to the Settecento had that feeling, the dread of emptiness, the dread, that is, of a world without God.

Sentimento del tempo is therefore the unappeasable fullness of the sun and, at the same time, in the second part of the book, the enclosure of man inside his own frailty. In *Sentimento del tempo*, as in any other moment of my poetry up to the present day, this man that I am, imprisoned in his own liberty, since like every other living being he is struck by the atonement for an obscure guilt, could not help but try to raise the presence of a dream of innocence. Of innocence before Adam, of the world before man. Dream from which it isn't known which other baptism would be able to redeem us, taking our minds off the persecution of memory.

[The following are Ungaretti's notes to this volume.]

Silenzio in Liguria/Silence in Liguria **PAGE 75**
I had gone to a conference in Genoa, invited by the French news agency Radio; it was
the time of [Luigi] Facta. My wife was representing another agency, we were in charge
of the information service of the conference. We were staying in a hotel in Nervi because
there was no place left in Genoa.
   [Luigi Facta was Italy's last prime minister before Mussolini took power.]

Sirene/Sirens **PAGE 77**
l. 1: *Deadly spirit*. It is inspiration, which is always ambiguous and contains in itself an
   incitement and an illusory truth, the restlessness of which was announced before-
   hand; it is the muse in the form of siren, and the fateful island is present in poetry, of
   course, the island of the sirens met by Ulysses in his voyage.
   [l. 3: *all' alto*. An archaism for *in alto mare*, "to high seas."]

Ricordo d'Affrica/Memory of Africa **PAGE 79**
ll. 8–9: *Nor . . . Diana / Stepping from the sparse palm grove*. Diana is, of course, the
   moon; a mythical personification also, in feminine form. In the poem there is the idea
   of mirage, since the effects of mirage are analogous to lunar ones.

L'isola/The Island **PAGE 81**
The landscape is Tivoli's. Why "the island"? Because it is the spot where I go for
solitude, where I am alone: it is a spot separate from the rest of the world, not because
it is that in reality but because in my state of mind there I can withdraw from every-
thing.

Lago luna alba notte/Lake Moon Dawn Night **PAGE 83**
The lake evoked is the one in Albano. [Albano is one of the *castelli romani*, near Marino.]

Inno alla morte/Hymn to Death **PAGE 85**
l. 5: (*At the foot of the ravine*. Once again the landscape of Tivoli, of the Villa Gregori-
   ana, at the moment in which night ends, as if everything had to end at that moment.
   [Villa Gregoriana is a park that commemorates Pope Gregory XVI; there's a huge
   waterfall there.]

Fine di Crono/End of Chronos **PAGE 97**
This poem is a fantasy of the end of the world. The stars, "countless Penelopes," spin life
until their Lord, their Ulysses, returns to embrace them, to annul them in himself. Then
Olympus will return, the absolute stillness, the no-longer-being-in-existence.

Con fuoco/With Fire **PAGE 99**

l. 1: *a homesick wolf*. The wolf, grown old and therefore nostalgic, but with the violence of youth in his desire, is the poet.

Ultimo quarto/Last Quarter **PAGE 101**

This poem describes a night spent in Tivoli, in front of Hadrian's Villa. The villa was closed, the watchman didn't want to let us in, and Jean Paulhan, Franz Hellens, our wives, and I scaled the wall and contemplated the unforgettable sight the poem alludes to. It may be that Hadrian's Villa, its piercing melancholy, manifests its uselessness, the powerlessness of reinstating that dream of an emperor burned by nostalgia, who had suggested erecting a sort of Greece in miniature, for his use and consumption, a few leagues from Rome. Nostalgia is at the heart of every manifestation of poetry, and Hadrian was a poet.

Il capitano/The Captain **PAGE 113**

l. 11: *Echoes from before my birth*. His own ancestors from Lucca.

l. 14: *And cast on rock*. Evocation of the landscape of war.

l. 18: We called him Cremona; his baptismal name was Nazzareno. He was a blond young man, very handsome, almost two meters tall, was a part of my regiment, and died, crushed, in the Carso.

La madre/The Mother **PAGE 117**

This poem was written on the occasion of my mother's death.

La pietà/Mercy **PAGE 121**

This poem was published for the first time, in a text translated by me, in *Nouvelle Revue Française*, in the place of honor, and given the historical moment, it aroused widespread disturbance. It is the first resolute manifestation of my return to the Christian faith, which, even if other aspirations first enticed me, never stopped waiting inside me, hidden. It was born during Holy Week, in the monastery of Subiaco, where I was a guest of my old friend Don Francesco Vignanelli, monk at Montecassino.

Caino/Cain **PAGE 129**

ll. 22–23: *Tedium's impudent daughter, / Memory*. Memory is the daughter of tedium because man has adapted himself to the toil of work, in order not to be aware of the tedium of life. It is "impudent" because it tries to mask tedium. Memory is history.

[*Il deserto e dopo: Prose di viaggio e saggi* (Mondadori, 1961; the subtitle is "Travel Prose and Essays") is a volume of poetic prose, mostly travel pieces, that Ungaretti wrote for the Turin newspaper *Gazzetta del Popolo*. He wrote them over a period of four years, from 1931 to 1934. This is why I've placed "The Laugh of the Djinn Rull" after *Sentimento*, which Ungaretti was finishing during this period. Some of these pieces, including the one in the current selection, were collected for the first time in 1949 by Mondadori, in a volume called *Il povero nella città* (The Poor Man in the City) and reprinted in *Il deserto e dopo*, which also included some of Ungaretti's translations from Brazilian popular poetry and song—that of Mario de Andrade, Manuel Bandeira, and others.]

The Laugh of the Djinn Rull PAGE 155
[The djinn Rull is a demon of death by thirst. Ungaretti wrote this prose piece, published as "La risata dello djinn Rull" in *Gazzetta del Popolo* on September 12, 1931, and others when he made his first trip back to Egypt in twenty years.]

IL DOLORE/AFFLICTION

Having lost a nine-year-old boy [his son, Antonietto, in 1939], I know that death is death in an extremely brutal way. It was the most terrible event of my life. I know what death means, I knew it even before; but then, when the best part of me was ripped away, I experienced death in myself, from that moment on. *Il dolore* is the book I love most, the book I wrote in the horrible years, a lump in my throat. It would strike me as shameless to talk about it. That pain will never stop tormenting me.

[In the original 1947 Mondadori edition of *Il dolore*, Ungaretti wrote:]

"Tutto ho perduto" was written in memory of my brother; Antonietto, my son, whom I lost in Brazil, is present in "Giorno per giorno" and in the group "Il tempo è muto"; in other poems, *Il dolore* is particularly inspired by the tragedy of these years.
   [The original of "Giorno per giorno" (Day by Day) has seventeen sections in all. The group "Il tempo è muto" is represented here by the poem with that name, "Time Is Silent," and "Tu ti spezzasti" (You Were Broken). The tragedy Ungaretti refers to at the end of this note is, of course, World War II.]

The original edition of *La terra promessa* was published by Arnoldo Mondadori, Milan, in 1950.

In order to appear a little less incomplete, the book ought to have included "Cori d'Enea" as well. *Il taccuino del vecchio* and "Ultimi cori per la Terra Promessa" might in some way represent the outline for it.

["Cori d'Enea" (Choruses of Aeneas) was a planned work that Ungaretti never completed. See pages 212–225 for a selection from "Ultimi cori per la Terra Promessa" (Last Choruses from the Promised Land).]

I had the first idea for *La terra promessa* in 1935, right after the composition of "Auguri per il proprio compleanno" [Greetings for His Own Birthday]. In that poem, in the last strophe, I said:

> Fleeting youth of the senses
> That keeps me in the dark about myself
> And allows the images to timelessness:
>
> Suffering, don't leave me, stay!

Again in 1942, when Mondadori began the publication of all my work, *La terra promessa* was announced by editorial leaflets with the name *Penultima stagione* [Next-to-Last Season]. It was autumn that I meant to sing in my poem, an already advanced autumn, from which the last sign of youth, the last fleshly appetite, takes its leave forever.

Canzone PAGE 199
"Canzone," which justifies the incomplete poem [as which *La terra promessa* had originally been conceived], takes as its starting point the separation, already mentioned, of autumn from the last sign of youth and gives as its first strophic moment an infinitesimally slow dissolution, almost imperceptible, an infinitesimally slow loss of memory in a lucid drunkenness. Then it is the rebirth to another level of reality: through reminiscence, it is the birth of the reality of the second level, it is the exhaustion of sensual experience, the crossing over the threshold of another experience, the penetrating into new experience, illusively and not illusively primal—it is the consciousness of being out of nonbeing, being out of nothingness, the Pascalian consciousness of being out of nothingness. Horrible consciousness. Its odyssey always takes the past as its point of departure, forever returns to a close in the past, forever leaves again from the same mental dawn, forever comes to a close in the same dawn of the mind.

"Canzone" is formed, as I was saying, following the transference of the sources of inspiration from the sphere of sensual reality to the sphere of intellectual reality. The wall between the two spheres, to tell the truth, is fluid; the two spheres interpenetrate. At a certain period of existence, one may have had the sensation that the mental in him excluded every other activity: the limit of age is limit. It is not limit, since poetry is never made without the senses' help as well, especially a poem of strict and infinite musical quality such as that which you will now enjoy reading tries to be.

Cori descrittivi di stati d'animo di Didone/
Choruses Descriptive of Dido's States of Mind PAGE 203
Nineteen choruses that would dramatically describe the departure of the last glimmers of youth from a person, or from a civilization, since even civilizations are born, grow, decline, and die. The intention here is to give the physical experience of the drama [of Dido's passion], with reappearances of happy moments, vague uncertainties, and alarmed senses of shame, in the middle of being delirious over a passion that is seen perishing and becoming repellent, desolating, deserted.

Variazioni su nulla/Variations on Nothing PAGE 209
The theme is earthly duration beyond the singularity of persons. Nothing but a disincarnate clock that, alone in the void, continues dripping the minutes.

IL TACCUINO DEL VECCHIO/
THE OLD MAN'S NOTEBOOK

[This book was published by Mondadori in 1960. From it, I've selected a little more than half the sections of "Ultimi cori per la Terra Promessa," plus a short poem, "Per sempre" (Forever).

I've combined *Il taccuino del vecchio, Dialogo,* and *Nuove* into one part of this book—and one collection from the early fifties, *Un grido e paesaggi* (An Outcry and Landscapes), isn't represented here at all—because they are actually quite slim volumes, with some often not very notable poems.]

Ultimi cori per la Terra Promessa/Last Choruses for the Promised Land PAGE 213
Choruses 1, 3, 24 were born from a brief return last year [1959] to Egypt with Leonardo Sinisgalli and were suggested in particular by the desert landscape of the necropolis of Sakkarah. A jet flight from Hong Kong to Beirut in the course of my recent trip to Japan with Jean Fautrier and Jean Paulhan provided the pretext for chorus 23. Other choruses

have their source in strictly personal events or events such as, in chorus 16, the launching of artificial satellites. They are all themes which, as far as the author is concerned, need not count as his own if he has succeeded in giving them life in poetry.

[There are a total of twenty-seven "choruses" in this sequence.]

Per Sempre/Forever PAGE 227
[This poem was written in memory of Ungaretti's wife of thirty-eight years, Jeanne Dupoix, who died in Rome in 1958.]

DIALOGO/DIALOGUE

This collection was published, in an edition of a few copies not for sale, on the occasion of my eightieth birthday, in February 1968. It is composed of my poems in which, realizing my age, I dare to point out that love can't be extinguished except by death.

[*Dialogo* was published by Editore Fògola in Turin. I've chosen four poems from it: "12 settembre 1966," "La conchiglia" (The Conch), "Il lampo della bocca" (The Flash of the Mouth), and "Superstite infanzia" (Surviving Childhood). Ungaretti's nine love poems were accompanied by five poem-replies—to be found in *Vita d'un uomo*—of a young Brazilian poetess, Bruna Bianco, with whom Ungaretti fell in love when he went to Brazil and Peru to receive honorary degrees in 1968.]

NUOVE / NEW THINGS

[*Nuove* is the section of *Vita d'un uomo* that contains Ungaretti's last poems—two, plus the three-part sequence "Croazia Segreta" (Secret Croatia).]

UNGARETTI ON UNGARETTI

[Published as the opening to the notes section of *Vita d'un uomo*, under the title "Nota introduttiva."]

p. 249: *The Capitulations.* An agreement whereby the rulers of Egypt allowed all foreigners and their children to derive their legal status from the country of their origin. This system of foreign protection, which originated under the Ottomans, came to be called the Laws of Capitulations.

Some of the contemporaries Ungaretti mentions in this selection are:

Louis Aragon (1897–1982), French Surrealist poet, novelist, and essayist
Giacomo Balla (1871–1958), Italian Futurist painter
Joseph Bédier (1864–1938), scholar of medieval French literature
Umberto Boccioni (1882–1916), Italian Futurist painter and sculptor
André Breton (1896–1966), French poet, critic, and chief promoter of Surrealism
Carlo Carrà (1881–1966), Italian Futurist painter
Henry Church (1887–?), American writer and editor
Robert Delaunay (1885–1941), French Cubist painter
Robert Desnos (1900–1945), French Surrealist poet
Léon-Paul Fargue (1876–1947), French poet and essayist
Bernard Groethuysen (1880–1946), French Marxist theorist and writer
Piero Jahier (1884–1966), Italian novelist
Valery-Nicolas Larbaud (1881–1957), French novelist and critic
Henri Michaux (1899–1984), Belgian-born French poet and painter
Enrico Pea (1881–1958), Italian novelist, playwright, and poet
Georges Sorel (1847–1922), French socialist and revolutionary syndicalist
Philippe Soupault (1897–1990), French Surrealist poet and novelist
Chaim Soutine (1894–1943), Russian-born French Expressionist painter
Tristan Tzara (1896–1963), Romanian-born French poet and essayist known mainly
    as the founder of Dada

Acknowledgments

Jonathan Galassi's sensitive and skillful editing was just what I needed to see through the blind spots in my translations and to see what else would make this book better. I've been extremely lucky to have his help, and I'm very grateful for his interest and belief in my project.

I was fortunate also to receive the comments of Professor Luciano Rebay, Giuseppe Ungaretti Professor in Italian Literature at Columbia University, whose marvelously knowledgeable reading of the text set me straight on quite a few points I'd missed or mistaken. I thank him for his help. Valentina Manieri's intelligent, caring native Italian reading of the manuscript was a godsend; many of her insights and suggestions are in this book. Anna Maria Farabbi's reading also was important to my understanding of the original text. Naturally, any infelicities that may remain in the translation are entirely my own doing.

Many other readers have helped, advised, or encouraged me. My thanks especially to Dana Gioia and Peter Russell; and to the people in the Somerville poetry group who read some of my first efforts, in particular Pam Greenberg and Page Nelson-Saginor. I'm grateful also to Stephen Dobyns, Brooks Haxton, and Mary Karr for their generosity when I was at Syracuse. And thanks to Peter Marcus for his pep talks and interest.

Earlier English-language translations of Ungaretti, by Allen Mandelbaum, Patrick Creagh, Kevin Hart, and Diego Bastianutti, were helpful references.

My thanks to Arnoldo Mondadori Editore, in Milan, and in particular to Emanuela Canali, foreign rights manager at Mondadori, for permission to publish my translations of Ungaretti.

James Wilson at Farrar, Straus and Giroux has been a pleasure to work with. He has guided this book through production with true style and flair.

Thanks also to Alfredo de Palchi and the NIAF Sonia Raiziss Giop Foundation Grant in Translating for support for this project; and to the editors of the following journals, in which earlier versions of some of these translations were published: *DoubleTake*, *International Poetry Review*, *Italian Americana*, *Modern Poetry in Translation*, *The New Republic*, *The New Yorker*, *Partisan Review*, *Tin House*, and *Yale Italian Poetry*. The introduction, "Giuseppe Ungaretti and the Image of Desolation," was first published in the *Hudson Review*, along with translations of five of the poems in this book: "Brothers," "Sunset," "With Fire," "Variations on Nothing," and "Last Choruses for the Promised Land" (parts 1, 5, 24, and 27).

My father gave me the beautiful Mondadori volumes of Ungaretti that have been such excellent company; and my mother's support and enthusiasm, as always, have made a huge difference. My father's wife, Phina Festa Frisardi, and my mother's husband, Vince Cleary, have also helped me out a lot along the way.

My wife, Daphne, has been a positively wonderful help, friend, and support throughout this project, encouraging me to do it in the first place and responding insightfully to most of the pieces as I went along. Her presence blessed and blesses this book.

Index of Titles and First Lines

(Page numbers in bold refer to the text; those in italics, following poem titles, refer to the notes.)

A casa mia, in Egitto, **6 8**

A conchiglia del buio **2 3 0**

A Riposo **2 0**, *265*

A una proda ove sera era perenne **8 0**

Accadrà? **1 8 4**

After I lost my father in 1890, **2 3 8**

Agglutinati, all'oggi **2 1 2**

Agonia **8**

Agony **9**

Allegria di naufragi **5 4**

Amaro accordo **1 7 6**

Amore, mio giovine emblema, **8 4**

An abandonment seizes me by the throat **2 3 7**

An entire night **1 9**

And promptly takes up **5 5**

And the trees and the night **1 5 1**

And when with a final beat my heart **1 1 7**

Another Night **5 7**

Appiè dei passi della sera **1 1 0**

At my house in Egypt, **6 9**

At the foot of evening's passage **1 1 1**

Attrito **4 8**

Auguri per il proprio compleanno **1 4 6**

Avido lutto ronzante nei vivi, **9 2**

Beautiful Night **4 5**

Between one flower plucked and the other given **5**

Bitter Harmony **1 7 7**

Bosco Cappuccio **3 2**

Brothers **3 1**

Cain **1 2 9**, *274*

Caino **1 2 8**, *274*

Canto **1 4 4**

Canzone **1 9 8**, **1 9 9**, *276*

C'era una volta **3 2**, *265*

Cessate d'uccidere i morti, **1 9 0**

Chi mi accompagnerà pei campi **2 0**

Chiuso fra cose mortali **2 4**

Choruses Descriptive of Dido's States of Mind, *from* **2 0 3**, *277*

Closed off among things that die **2 5**

Come allodola ondosa **1 1 8**

Come dolce prima dell'uomo **1 3 2**

Commiato **5 2**, *266*

Con fuoco **9 8**, *274*

Con fuoco d'occhi un nostalgico lupo **9 8**

Con la mia fame di lupo **4 8**

Cori descrittivi di stati d'animo di Didone, *from* **2 0 2**, *277*

Corre sopra le sabbie favolose **1 2 8**

D'agosto 9 2
Dall'ampia ansia dell'alba 7 2
Dalla spoglia di serpe 9 4
DAMNATION 2 5
DANNAZIONE 2 4
DAY BY DAY, from 1 6 7
Deadly spirit 7 7
Dear 5 3
DEATH MEDITATED ON 1 3 7
Delicate bushes, cilia 8 3
Di che reggimento siete 3 0
DI LUGLIO 8 8
D'improvviso 6 4
Di queste case 4 6
12 SETTEMBRE 1966 2 2 8
Dolce declina il sole. 1 4 6
DOVE LA LUCE 1 1 8

E gli alberi e la notte 1 5 0
E il cuore quando d'un ultimo battito 1 1 6
E subito riprende 5 4
EARTH 1 9 3
END OF CHRONOS 9 7, 273
ENVOI 5 3, 266
ETERNAL 5
ETERNO 4
EVENING 1 1 1
Evening having arrived, 1 0 7
Evening is prolonged by hanging fire 2 0 3
Ever stretched in anguish 1 8 5
EVERY GRAY 9 5

Fermato a due sassi 4 2
FINE DI CRONO 9 6, 273
For a God who laughs like a child, 1 4 9
FOREVER 2 2 7, 278
FRATELLI 3 0

FRICTION 4 9
From serpent's slough 9 5
Fui pronto a tutte le partenze. 1 1 2
Funesto spirito 7 6

Gentile 5 2
GENTLY THE SUN GOES DOWN. 1 4 7
GIORNO PER GIORNO, from 1 6 6
Gioventù impietrita, 1 0 2
GIROVAGO 6 6, 267
GIUGNO 5 3, 267
GIUNONE 9 0
Giunta la sera, 1 0 6
Gracili arbusti, ciglia 8 2
GREETINGS FOR HIS OWN BIRTHDAY
    1 4 7
GRIDO 1 0 6

Halted at two boulders 4 3
He landed on a waterfront where evening 8 1
He runs across the fabulous sands 1 2 9
His name was 1 3
How lovely the world must have been 1 3 3
HYMN TO DEATH 8 5, 273

I am a poet 5 1
I am a wounded man. 1 2 1
I FIUMI 3 4, 265
I hang on to this mangled tree 3 5
I molti, immani, sparsi, grigi sassi 1 7 8
I see your slow mouth again 1 4 5
I was always ready for departures. 1 1 3
If you came back alive to meet me, 1 6 5
IF YOU MY BROTHER 1 6 5
If you, my dear, should hold 2 3 1
IL CAPITANO 1 1 2, 274
Il carnato del cielo 2 2

Il cielo pone in capo 10
IL LAMPO DELLA BOCCA 234
IL PORTO SEPOLTO 16
IL TEMPO È MUTO 174
Il tempo è muto fra canneti immoti . . . 174
In agguato 40
IN AUGUST 93
In Cappuccio Forest 33
IN JULY 89
IN MEMORIA 12
IN MEMORY OF 13
In nessuna 66
In quest'oscuro 56
In this darkness 57
IN VEINS 183
In veins already almost empty tombs 183
INNO ALLA MORTE 84, 273
ITALIA 50
ITALY 51
I'VE LOST ALL 163
I've lost all of childhood; 163

JOY OF SHIPWRECKS 55
JUNE 59, 267
JUNO 91

LA CONCHIGLIA 230
La linea 6
LA MADRE 116, 274
LA MORTE MEDITATA 136
LA NOTTE BELLA 44
LA PIETÀ 120, 274
LA PREGHIERA 132
La sera si prolunga 202
LAGO LUNA ALBA NOTTE 82, 273
LAKE MOON DAWN NIGHT 83, 273
L'ANGELO DEL POVERO 188

LAST CHORUSES FOR THE PROMISED
  LAND, *from* 213, 277
LAST QUARTER 101, 275
LEVANT 7, 265
LEVANTE 6, 265
Like a skylark on its airy way 119
L'ISOLA 80, 273
L'ora impaurita 96
Love, my youthful emblem, 85
LUCCA 68, 69, 267
Luna, 100
L'uva è matura, il campo arato, 108

MAY NIGHT 11
MEMORY OF AFRICA 79, 273
MERCY 121, 274
Mi tengo a quest'albero mutilato 34
Migliaia d'uomini prima di me, 234
MONOTONIA 42
MONOTONY 43
Moon, 101
Morire come le allodole assetate 8
My every moment 27

NELLE VENE 182
Nelle vene già quasi vuote tombe 182
No more now will I go off alone 79
NON GRIDATE PIÙ 190
Non più ora tra la piana sterminata 78
Nothing is left 47
NOTTE DI MAGGIO 10
Now that the harsher mercy of blood and earth
  189
Nude, le braccia di segreti sazie, 198

O NIGHT 73
O NOTTE 72

O sister of shadow, 137

O sorella dell'ombra, 136

OGNI GRIGIO 94

Ogni mio momento 26

ONCE UPON A TIME 33, 265

Only in dreams now can I kiss 167

Oppure in un meriggio d'un ottobre 176

Or at noontime on an October day 177

Ora che invade le oscurate menti 188

Ora potrò baciare solo in sogno 166

Out of daybreak's huge and restless hunger 73

OUTCRY 107

PELLEGRINAGGIO 40, 266

PER SEMPRE 226, 278

Per un Iddio che rida come un bimbo, 148

Petrified youth, 103

PILGRIMAGE 41, 266

Potrebbe esserci sulla falce 192

PRAYER 133

Quale canto s'è levato stanotte 44

Quando 58

Quando su ci si butta lei, 88

Quel nonnulla di sabbia che trascorre 208

QUIETE 108

REAWAKENINGS 27

RESTING 21, 265

RICORDO D'AFFRICA 78, 273

RISVEGLI 26

Rivedo la tua bocca lenta 144

SAN MARTINO DEL CARSO 46, 47

Scade flessuosa la pianura d'acqua. 74

Se tu mi rivenissi incontro vivo, 164

SE TU MIO FRATELLO 164

SECRET CROATIA, *from* 238

Sei comparsa al portone 228

Senza niuna impazienza sognerò, 226

SENZA PIÙ PESO 148

SEPTEMBER 12, 1966 229

SERA 110

SHOUT NO MORE 191

Si chiamava 12

SILENCE IN LIGURIA 75, 273

SILENZIO IN LIGURIA 74, 273

SILENZIO STELLATO 150

SIRENE 76, 273

SIRENS 77, 273

So round and full it drives me mad, 91

SONG 145

Sono un poeta 50

Sono un uomo ferito. 120

STARRY SILENCE 151

STARS 105

STATUA 102

STATUE 103

STELLE 104

STILLNESS 109

Stop killing the dead, 191

Suddenly 64

SUNSET 23

SUPERSTITE INFANZIA 236

SURVIVING CHILDHOOD 237

TERRA 192

Tesa sempre in angoscia 184

That negligible bit of sand which slides 209

THE BURIED HARBOR 17

THE CAPTAIN 113, 274

THE CONCH 231

The days that are past 213
The fables are in flames again up high.
105
THE FLASH OF THE MOUTH 235
The flesh-pink of the sky 23
The grapes are heavy, the field plowed,
109
THE ISLAND 81, 273
THE LAUGH OF THE DJINN RULL 155,
275
The many, gigantic, jumbled, glaucous stones
179
THE MOTHER 117, 274
The poet arrives there 17
THE POOR MAN'S ANGEL 189
The puffy line 7
THE RIVERS 35, 265
The sky arranges garlands 11
The strange and frightened moment 97
The sun is already sinking 155
The supple plain of water dwindles. 75
There is no 67
There might be a shining 193
Those bare arms surfeited with secrets have,
199
Thousands of men before me, 235
TIME IS SILENT 175
Time is silent among motionless rushes . . .
175
To die like skylarks thirsty 9
Tonda quel tanto che mi dà tormento,
90
Tornano in alto ad ardere le favole. 104
Tra un fiore colto e l'altro donato 4
TRAMONTO 22
Trapped 41
TU TI SPEZZASTI 178

TUTTO HO PERDUTO 162
Tutto ho perduto dell'infanzia 162

ULTIMI CORI PER LA TERRA PROMESSA,
from 212, 277
ULTIMO QUARTO 100, 274
Un abbandono mi afferra alla gola 236
UN'ALTRA NOTTE 56
Un'intera nottata 18

VANITÀ 64
VANITY 65
VARIATIONS ON NOTHING 209, 277
VARIAZIONI SU NULLA 208, 277
VEGLIA 18
Vi arriva il poeta 16
VIGIL 19
Voracious mourning buzzing in the living,
93

WANDERER 67, 267
WEIGHTLESS 149
What regiment are you from 31
What song has risen tonight 45
When 59
When she hurls herself on it headlong, 89
WHERE THE LIGHT 119
Who will come with me through the fields
21
WILL IT COME TO PASS? 185
WITH FIRE 99, 274
With fire in his eyes a homesick wolf 99
With my wolf's hunger 49
Without impatience I'll dream, 227

You showed up at the door 229
YOU WERE BROKEN 179

Made in the USA
San Bernardino, CA
25 June 2019